The Living Underground

The Living Underground
A Critical Overview
by
Hugh Fox

Whitston Publishing Company
Incorporated
Troy, New York
1970

Contents

In respect to *The Living Underground,* I am grateful for permissions from the authors, except where publishers permissions are noted, to quote pertinent material from the following publications:

Douglas Blazek. *Ole Anthology.* Glendale, California: Poetry X/Change Press, 1967.
—*Life in a Common Gun.* Madison, Wisconsin: Quixote Press, 1968.
—*Sting & Die.* Eugene, Oregon: Toad Press, 1968.
—*I Advance with a Loaded Rose.* San Francisco: Twowindows Press, 1969.

George Brecht. *Chance-Imagery.* New York: Something Else Press, 1966. With the permission of the publisher.

Don Cauble. *Inside Out.* Portland, Oregon: Dead Angel Press, 1968.
—*Early Morning Death Fragments,* ed. T. L. Kryss. Cold Mountain Publishing Company, 1969.

Joel Deutsch. *Space Heaters.* San Francisco: Open Skull Press, 1969.

Dick Higgins. *Jefferson's Birthday/Postface.* New York: Something Else Press, 1964.
—*A Book about Love & War and Death, Cantos 2 and 3.* San Francisco: Nova Broadcast Press, 1969.
—*foew&ombwhnw.* New York: Something Else Press, 1969. With permission of the publisher.

Brown Miller. *Fertilized Brains: Prayers and Profanities* San Francisco: Open Skull Press, 1968.
—*Thirty-Three Phases of the Fatal Stroboscope.* Sacramento, California: Runcible Spoon Press, 1968.
—*Autopsies and Family Ghosts.* Sacramento, California: Runcible Spoon Press, 1969.
—*Waters and Shadows.* San Francisco: Twowindows Press, 1969.

—*Whiskeytown Iron Mountain Triptych.* Death Crater, California; Molly Moon Press, 1969.

—*Yes, We are Living in this Ocean (A Word Mosaic).* Death Crater, California: Molly Moon Press, 1969.

Richard Morris. *He Dreamed,* published as *Quark,* no. 2. Reno, Nevada, 1967.

—*Prey.* Portland, Oregon: Wine Press, 1968.

—*Don Giovanni Meets the Lone Ranger.* Cleveland, Ohio: Posit Ion Press, 1968.

—*Ginsburg Smoked Some Dope and Einstein Played His Violin.* East Lansing, Michigan: Ghost Dance Press, 1970.

John Oliver Simon. *Roads to Dawn Lake.* Berkeley, California: Oyez, 1968.

—*Dancing Bear.* Berkeley, California: Undermine Press, 1969.

D. r. Wagner. *Book for Barb.* Berkeley, California: Undermine Press, 1967.

—*The Footsteps of the Returning King that Have Been Lost to Us so Long it Seems like They Never and Other Poems.* Sacramento, California: Runcible Spoon Press, 1968.

—*Putah Creek Overflow.* Sacramento, California: Runcible Spoon Press, 1968.

—*The Sirens in the Park and the Ribbons in the Hairs.* Folsom, California: Grande Ronde Press, 1968–1969.

—*AMPER&AND* [anthology]. San Francisco, California: Black Rabbit Press, 1969.

—*Panama Gold.* Sacramento & San Francisco: Black Rabbit Press, 1969.

Introduction

In the U.S. today there are really two cultures, one massive, massively distributed, saturating the mass media, universally known, and accepted, an integral, necessary, functional part of U.S. mass culture. The name studios in Hollywood, the name television networks, the big commercial magazines and newspapers, the name record companies, the Madison and Fifth Avenue publishers all produce *Entertainment as a Commercial Product*. Or—increasingly—as a *Commercial By-Product*. In TV, for example, the space between commercials is subordinate to the commercials themselves and a "literary magazine" like *The New Yorker* is mostly ads, with a short story or two, some commentary, some cartoons, a couple of light poems. Newspapers have become "news between ads." Ironically enough, Hollywood, while at the same time the cheapest, most commercial of the mass media outlets, still is the "purest." You go to a movie and you may see life reduced to its commonest demoninator for a common denominator mass-audience, but at least the movie is there as a pure, uninterrupted art-form. The popcorn and hotdog business in the lobby ends at the door. For the most part this is also true of that dying art-form, the printed book, which, in the hands of the U.S. big-business mentality has been turned into a slick, well-written, attractive, in fact tantalizing product which like Klennex or Schlitz Beer invites you to pick it up, feel it, buy it and use it . . . . maybe not all of it, of course (who reads an *entire* book nowadays?), but at least to sample and be able to sum it up.

The older "forms," then, the movie and the book, have become the least commercialized, and the newest "forms," radio and TV, have become the most. Whatever still-uninvented form that might be invented in the near future will most certainly be totally treated as a product-sales medium, and any non-product, non-commercial aspects will be tolerated rather than encouraged.

At the same time on TV the ad has become an art form. The selling of products has become the slickest, fastest, most attractive art-form coming out of the U.S. today.

Simultaneous with the total commercial perfection of new "forms" like radio and TV, one offshoot of the older "forms" (books and movies) has experienced a radically different development which is diametrically opposed not only to commercialization in the form of ads (product-sales), but also to the reduction of art to its lowest, common, mass-appeal denominator.

In a sense the development of a U.S. underground press and film world is a result of industrial "waste." Printing techniques such as offset or mimeo have simplified all printing processes, and film techniques have been increasingly simplified and reduced in cost, but the fact is that in an industrial society that is almost always on the brink of overproduction, second-hand machines are easy to come by, and it is possible to acquire printing and movie equipment for a fraction of its original cost.

In the early 1950's, because of the wave of prosperity that followed the second world war, because of the G.I. Bill, because of a new aura of affluence in the U.S., because of the Bomb and the imminence of total nuclear destruction, because of the expansion and improvement of the U.S. university system, and because the U.S. commercial system had become increasingly a straight jacket and a prisoncell, the Beat Revolution took place and brought a new kind of

writer into the U.S. literary scene: a Jack Kerouac, and
Allen Ginsberg, John Clellon Holmes, Lawrence Ferlinghetti.

Poetry, by the fifties, had become a sadly academic affair.
It wasn't really commercial. It wouldn't sell cars. It wasn't
really "visual" enough for TV, and publishing houses in New
York brought out their poets dutifully in small editions more
because of habit than need or even taste. Poetry itself had
become "neat" and clean: Karl Shapiro, Randall Jarrell, and
of course the grand old man of U.S. poetry, Robert Frost.

Then came the revolution: Ginsberg, Kerouac, Lamantia,
John O'Hara, Chandler Bossard, John Clellon Holmes,
Seymour Krim, Diana DePrima. Artificial, theoretical
academic language went out the window and subjectwise the
poets and novelists left the universities and the libraries, went
out into the streets, up into the mountains, into the bedrooms
and toilets, and rediscovered America—this time a personal,
essential, secretion and emotion centered America which was
real, multi-dimensional, raw, insulting and totally unexpected.

Kerouac in *On the Road* and Ginsberg in *Howl* created a
new poet-image for the twentieth-century: coarse, experience-
oriented, at the same time spiritual, idealistic, even mystical.
The orient was imported and spliced on to a kind of neo-
Transcendentalism a la Thoreau and Emerson. The new voice
decried American materialism, and chanted "Sutras." If the
Beats were bums, they were "Dharma Bums," stripped of the
accoutrements of the bourgeoise in order to seek and find
Enlightenment. They rediscovered the American Indian and
made the "noble Savage" even more noble than he had ever
been. They weren't interested in time-clocks, schedules,
"making it" in the old, traditional American sense, but in
discovering who they were, what they were, where they and
their country were going.

Lawrence Ferlinghetti in San Francisco started City Lights
books and actually made money with Ginsberg's *Howl,* and
showed that, yes, it was possible to have a publishing house

outside New York, and that, yes, a publishing alternative was possible. Little mags sprang up everywhere, and the New York-centrism of "the literary world" shafted out westward and the possibilities of multiple alternatives grew.

The entire current underground literary scene in the U.S. is a direct development of the breakthrough that the Beats had started. City Lights, of course, still continues on, and Ferlinghetti has also been publishing the *City Lights Review,* one of the better of the little magazines. San Francisco, where it all began, is still one of the focal points of "neo-Beat" (now "Hippy") literary activity, and in the last few years many young poet-editors have gone west from other parts of the U.S. to form a kind of "colony" in the Bay Area. Three prime examples: Doug Blazek (editor of Open Skull Press, originally from Bensonville, Illinois) and D. R. Wagner (now in Sacramento, California, originally from up-state New York, head of the Runcible Spoon Press), Jerry Burns (originally from Tampa, Florida, head of the Goliards Press). In the last year, though, there has been some movement away from San Francisco. Blazek is now in Sacramento, and Burns just moved up to Oregon.

Spiritually the link between this new generation and the Beats is nicely expressed by the Cleveland poet, D. A. Levy, who committed suicide last year. In his "Poem for Lama Ginsberg" (in *Ukanhavyrfuckincitibak*) he writes: "Everyone is following yr vision Allen."

Now, though, the Beat Revolution has become stabilized, permanent, perhaps even a kind of "establishment." There is COSMEP, the Cooperative of Small Magazine Editors and Presses, and the Underground News Syndicate. Dustbooks publishers an annual *Directory of Little Magazines,* and *Trace* magazine continues to publish its "evolving directory" of literary magazines. Now (again Dustbooks) there is even a *Small Press Review* dedicated solely to little magazines.

Luckily the Underground refuses to be entirely codified, catalogued, mummified and put in glass cases. The rebellion remains rebellious because new rebels keep entering into the fight: Tim Hildebrand, editor of *Mandala* (Madison Wisconsin), Jeff Woodward, editor of *Roots Forming* (Monroe, Michigan), Richard Krech of *Avalanche* (Berkeley), John Oliver Simon of the *Aldebaran Review* (Berkeley); and also, the old editors, some of them at least, refuse to let themselves fossilize. They don't sell out, continue "amateur" and free, don't commercialize, don't give in and fall down worshipping the Golden Calf of North America: success, spelled out bright and clear in noon or on the mosaiced pattern of a TV screen, editors like Duane Locke (*Poetry Review,* Tampa), Marvin Malone (*Wormwood Review,* Stockton, California), or Morris Edelson (*Quixote,* Madison, Wisconsin, in Warsaw, Poland this year).

And, thanks to mimeo and offset, whenever a young poet is not satisfied with the Underground scene the way it is, he can always start his own NEW magazine, often with a five hundred dollar grant from the Coordinating Council of Literary Magazines in New York, which has been set up precisely for that purpose.

The overriding characteristic of this Neo-Beat poetry is its realism, its realistic approach to contemporary life and experience. Douglas Blazek's statement in *Life in a Common Gun* more or less stands for most of the new poets:

> i describe & write abt what i know & what
> i've experienced hoping this writing will act
> as an internal catalyst to push myself further,
> develop the negative & help me grow, my ideal
> of what life should be is rarely expressed in
> writing because i really don't *know* that ideal,
> yet in my daily life i constantly strive for this
> ideal as in my dreams i try to feel its intensity &
> live its beauty.

The new American poetry, though, isn't all hard, concrete reality. The reality is there but the American, the inveterate idealist, can never accept merely *what's there,* always moves, like Blazek himself, toward an unformulated, inarticulate but everpresent idea of the ideal. Scratch the surface of a neo-Beat, neo-Naturalist, and you'll almost always find a neo-Transcendentalist, a neo-Romantic. Kerouac in *On the Road, The Dharma Bums, Doctor Sax, The Subterraneans,* was always an idealist in search of God, and what is Blazek's dream of Superman in his "Elegy for Superman" but another version of this quest for the transcendental:

O, Superman,
I woke up crying
   the night I read of your suicide—
you, wanting to *exceed* Superman
 & a million
   Lois Lane-eyed kids
 secure because we knew
   badmen were always caught
& there was no such
thing as working
   in a factory
     or being married.
(from *I Advance with a Leaded Rose*)

Sharon Asselin, wild, uncontrolled, always on the edge of suicide, revelation, a love-transfiguration, writes an elliptical poetry that is at the same time condensed, fragmentary and existentially essential. Her main topic: love-sex, her most important book to date *Return to Earth.* Steve Barfield, Richard Collier, and Sylvia Krohn are all members of the Tampa School of poetry and like the founder of the Tampa school, Duane Locke, are imagistically, surrealistically involved with a very distinctive aspect of American reality: the decaying old South invaded by a new industrial mystique. James Bertoline, Madison, Wisconsin, editor of the magazine *Abraxas,* author of *Day of Change* and *Drool* involves himself with the horror mixed in the ingredients of everyday life, the imminence of violence and blood always just beyond the pale of the everyday. He goes out, empties the garbage, comes back in and finds his girl bleeding from an abortion:

her red spattered my air, heart spinning
to seventy-eight
and over and flailing, still
in her pink Christmas robe, revealing

the terrible tools
probing her delicate depths—
("Revolutions Per Minute")

Hollace Cross from Columbia, Missouri, recent drug-crack-up, was editor of *Monument* magazine, writes in long Faulk-nerian lines about "the scene" in such a way that "the scene" becomes all scenes. He begins with the old values—honor, family, family love, ties, the need for purpose and ideals—and microscopes in on the contemporary world and sees how much that world lacks anything of permanent worth.

Joel Deutsch, now in San Francisco, author of *Give Me All Your Aces,* published by a press whose name he invented, the Lone Ranger Biology Press, now publishing a new magazine, *Meatball,* writes about trivialities, new shoes, tearing down old houses, his wife's beauty, his own paralysis and sense of worthlessness . . . . and everything he writes comes out sensitive, carefully honed, profound.

George Hitchcock and Robert Bly are two variations on the same theme: a kind of sur-real, un-real imagism that really represents a transition between the pre-Beat academics and the contemporary Neo-Beat movement. They are both "older," in their forties, not their twenties. Bly is the author of *The Light Around the Body,* published by Wesleyan University Press, and is editor of *The Sixties.* Hitchcock, editor of *Kayak,* is the author of *The Dolphin With the Revolver in Its Teeth.* Both are still barely in the Underground and are slowly passing into the Overground where they will be feted, embalmed and stored in libraries.

Brown Miller, another San Franciscan, is part of the Blazek-Asselin crowd, writes a poetry that is for the most part traditional syntactically and concerned with twisted, Poe-like explorations of human (especially family) relations. He is atavistic, iconoclastic, and enjoys his excremental vision of the universe:

> Afterwards, ignore my
> stagnant corpse
> if you can.
> Meanwhile, I eat old ladies
> and spice my suace with
> swirls of sea gulls
> caught in panther air.
> ("Final Data & Bleak Celebrations")

T. L. Kryss, from Cleveland, writes a hard-edged poetry that cuts like a razor, but at the same time, like D. R. Wagner in Sacramento, at times his idealism takes over and his vision emerges in infantile optimism:

> at dawn
> I look out the window
> at dark houses across the alley
> I light
> one red candle
> and watch
> as the clouds change music
>
> peace on my planet to
> animals of no will.
> (from *Look at the Moon, then Wipe the Light from Your
> Eyes and Tell Me What You See*)

Sometimes this optimism among the young subterraneans is drug-based. Blazek isn't a "user," but Richard Krech, author of the Rimbaud-like hallucinogenic poem, *The Hashish Scarab,* is, and he, like some of the other Berkeley poets, Charlie Potts (recently reborn as Laffing Water) and John Oliver Simon, have been looking to marijuna (and other hallucinogenics) as the solution to Western, Cartesian dualism, and imagine that the Era of Marijuna (Hashish) will force man out of his neurotically abstract pre-occupation with future and past and force him totally into the sanity of the new:

> after the legalization era
> there was several hundred years
> of enlightenment.
>
> however that is where
> the records leave
> off.
>   showing total
> pre-occupation
> with the
>
> present.
> *(The Hashish Scarab)*

D. A. Levy, before he committed suicide in 1968, was moving into a new kind of poetic development: purely visual, photographic collages, sound-poems, concrete poetry where the words merely serve as a visual matrix for the formation of "forms." This "pure form," total-visualization poetry is much more common outside of than inside of the U.S. because the U.S. poet still looks upon himself as a prophet. The medium for him isn't as important as the message. He has a scripture to announce, a visionary function to perform.

There are a few U.S. underground poets, though, who have latched onto the Dadaistic-Concrete line, and who have more or less given up message-preaching in the traditional sense, have turned to the evangelism of the absurd. Like San Diego poet, Lynn Lonidier, who in *Po Tree* writes:

> OPPS
> PADOOPE
> JOINT
> LABORATORY
> ACTION
> PARDON
> PARTNER-WALLOPED
> BALOOM BAAALOOM BAAAALOOO

Or Dick Higgins, founder of Something Else Press in New York whose poetry is discontinuous, perverse, multi-genred and multi-medied. He calls his latest book, *Foew&ombwhnw,* for example, not poetry, prose, theater or even a "collection," but "a grammar of the mind and a phenomenology of love and a science of the arts as seen by a stalker of the wild mushroom."

A typical poem of atypical Higgins is his "New Song in an Old Style":

<pre>
                         (check one)
                         ———— speak
                         ———— dance
    When I   ———— fall in love
                         ———— grow up
                         ———— grow old

                      (check one)
                              ———— I'm going to be
                              ———— it'll be with
                                        (check one)
                                        ———— an apple.
    ————   a lover.
                                        a smile.
                                        you.
</pre>

More typical of the underground scene is a kind of poetry that is strongly slanted toward the socio-economic. The Beat Revolt was, after all, basically a revolt against the paralyzing suffocation of middle class values, and in the hands of these neo-Beats, the revolt continues much along the same lines. Like Charlie Potts (Laffing Water's) poem "15 Days in the Middle Class:"

> my family tried to own two cars
> my brother and my sister split
> they helped me thru college
> nothing worked
> their marriage paint

peeled off a white house
(from *Little Lord Shiva*)

Nothing more vividly illustrates the split in the U.S. between the commercial (Overground) and non-commercial (Underground) cultures, than the fact that this whole world of underground magazines and poets is almost totally unknown by the U.S. public. Libraries for the most part don't subscribe to underground magazines, bookstores don't stock them . . . . there isn't really any place to find them. There are little magazine collections at the University of Wisconsin and Brown University (Harris Collection), and the Gotham Book Mart, Phoenix Book Store, and the Eighth Street Book Store in New York stock them (and there are scattered little mag bookstores throughout the U.S.), but for the most part the Underground stays underground and rarely sees the light of the commercial day, while the Overground continues to grind out books and magazines tailored to SELL.

This split in the little mag-poet world, though, is merely symptomatic of a total split in U.S. culture. The Old Culture, the academy, the closed corporation, the "serious" book or the "serious" concert, has given way to the New Pop Culture which, while being partially commercialized and incorporated into the U.S. marketing structure, at the same time has spawned a phantom, through-the-looking-glass, obverse-side-of-the-coin culture which is Pop in the sense that it touches the realities of American life, but which at the same time has not been absorbed into the bloodstream of the mass-media monster.

This other alternate culture resists incorporation into the slick-surfaced, mass-produced commercial U.S. world. For many of the underground poets, even COSMEP is too much of an "institution," too much of a "computer." The Underground WANTS to remain rough, poor, isolated within its own members. In a recent note to me D. R. Wagner wrote that he'd gotten out of COSMEP because it was getting to be too "efficient." The real Underground wants to remain inefficient, because efficiency too often means standardization and standardization means the complete loss of individuality. The Underground is the last stand of the individual in a demographically nightmarish world where "selfness" is defined as a betrayal of the "common good."

The movies, as the oldest among the new media forms, is having an interesting effect on the Underground. First of all, the walls between genres are being demolished. Theater, film, painting, poetry are all being combined to create supra generic, mixed media art forms.

The young American artist, still in his embryonic, developmental state, when he is first "artist" and feels the need for expression that the word "artist" connotes, before he has committed himself to any particular expressive mode, has a number of new fields open to him. He is not confined to either poetry or painting or even film, but can mix and combine various genres to suit his own needs.

At the same time film as such is in a sense attracting some artists who a few decades ago might easily have become poets. In his prophetic pamphlet entitled *Towards the 1970's,* Dick Higgins writes:

> . . . . the cinema is an art which captures its subject matter. Therefore the kinds of forms which were developed in poetry and Happenings in the 1960's can easily be adapted to structure objective bodies of subject matter. In this way also the cinema seems peculiarly timely as a medium. In the 1970's the elite artists will not be the visual ones, in all likelihood, but the film-makers and the choreographers. Both arts use time. And, for now, that seems to be the name of the game.

Many of the newer, fresher, more vital U.S. poets show in their works a determined direction toward increased plasticity and mobility that to me seems to be a kind of indirect, almost sub-conscious influence of the media revolution. Levy's last work was strongly in the direction of collage, D. R. Wagner's most recent work is totally graphics-art oriented, Kryss does a lot of work in silk screen, even Blazek has been working recently in prints.

Perhaps the most advanced case of media inter-penetration, though, is that of Lynn Lonidier in San Diego. Lynn's roomate is Pauline Oliveros, the electronic musician, and the two of them work together in producing light shows. Pauline on sound, Lynn on lights. Like Dick Higgins, Lynn also does films; her latest is *The Mummy in Southern California.*

All the new poets, though, in varying degrees experience some degree of media-influence, and as the media slowly replace the printed page—perhaps altogether—one can expect both an increasing disregard for genres as such, plus an increased use of film, TV, records, etc. as the most viable, vital modes of contemporary expression. The present generation hasn't been raised on books, TV could have been *the* key expressive mode of our times if it had had any *content,* but instead it hypnotizes young people up to a certain age and then a fragment breaks away and moves into records, lightshows, experimental movies, where the real action is. "Folkmusic" has been one of the real poetrys of our times . . . . the page has been replaced by guitar and voice . . . . we return to a direct, tribal communication mode, in a way very similar to the increased concentration of poetry readings.

The problem, of course, is how the unaffluent poet can utilize the electronic tools of his affluent surroundings. Film is somewhat open, records and tapes a bit less, TV still for the most part remains closed. At any rate, the impulse and direction are there; the only questition now is how to integrate the various genres to produce one, unified art form.

We can expect in the near future much less concentration on the "permanence" of any art expression. A light show, a happening, can happen once and then never happen again. The demographic explosion, accompanied as it is by the educational explosion drowns the individual artist in an over-sophisticated ambience of too many magazines, too many books, too many movies, too much to see, absorb, understand; and the accumulative quantity of worldwide art production automatically reduces perdurability, makes practically all art an evanescent, one-time "happening."

Moving away from durable materials such as paper, wood, stone, we move into an art of electronic impulses which is essentially impermanent. The solidity of expressive-mode dissolves and we are left with a tape that needs re-activation to be seen again. Our art becomes pure energy, for the new, for this instant, instilled with an instantaneous discontinuous rhythm.

Poetry is moving in this direction, toward an annihilation of its definable nature as poetry and its incorporation into a new kind of omni-art, a synthesis of all sense-experience, all communication within the unifying field of electronic expression. We are really still in the Stone Age of another historical cycle that is moving inexorably toward the development of a totally actualized electronic art.

D. A. Levy: An Overview

Levy's search was a sincere search for the genuine, eschewing all the pseudo-visionaries and their visions, reaching beyond anyone else's version of reality to reach his own—even if it killed him, which it did.

Death and emptiness are favorite associations. The press he was associated with was the Ghost Press, 7 Flowers Press, later Ghost Flower Press. His most important poems are *The North American Book of the Dead* and *Tombstone as a Lonely Charm*. His best friend, R J Sigismund (known simply as rjs); continues from Ground Zero and calls himself Captain Zero.

Ghost, Ghost Flower, Death, Tombstones. . . . Levy divests himself of all the trappings of "movements" in the great country of packaging and reduction to a common denominator, and distrusting all easy labels and simple solutions, makes his life a pilgrimage in search of the true truth, the genuine genuine, the real real.

The result was a series of "illuminations," a progression of visions, full of light and life . . . . but that ran down, ran back to the zero starting point, death:

    i am tired
      (wind)
    im sitting here

out of cigarettes
last week i turned on with peyote
        7 didn't turn on
i am tired
        (help its dark in here &
        im running out of matches)
tonight i feel like a corpse
        a child of ashes
        end of letter
but no poems lady berge'
the wind is carrying me away
("Letter to Lady Berge' " 2/27/66)

In a sense Levy is talking about himself in his poem for
Thom Szuter "Thinking of Rimbaud:" "stole from the
sun/bank & shot himself."
Perhaps the visionary quest began simply as beat-hip rebellion against the establishment. Levy's original press name
was, after all, Renegade Press, and there is more of the renegade than the visionary in many of Levy's anti-establishment
declarations, like the one, for example, that appeared in the
Marijuana Quarterly, Vol. 2, No. 1:

In 59 & 60 . . . . the first wave of the
'Beat Generation' had passed away . . . .
it arrived in cleveland's primitive
west side . . . . i stopped . . . . & looked
around & wondered . . . why? with all this
happening . . . . why? wasn't anything happening
in cleveland. Before I learned how to
swear & how this form of slow death of
a dead city can kill you before you know
it . . . I planned to change it.

Even beginning as a renegade, though, Levy never identified with other renegades, never saw himself as a part of any
renegade movement or tradition. He doesn't want to be beat
or hip or bourgeoise-gone-hip or anything else regularized or

categorized. He is isolated from *everything* and even his mysticism is an imperfect shield against the yahoo world that surrounds him: "Buddha or not, there is no time to sleep or loiter. Light does not make one immune from the blind gropings of dark minds." ("Notes/Variations on a Short Poem")

Levy's unique individuality, the real basis of his spiritual integrity, the core-value of his work, was not something that he came by easily, but something which he had to work at. He had to go back and "re-make" his whole psychological orientation, and he was constantly on guard for psychic detours, traps, mirages. "If you want a revolution," he says in Part III of *Tomb Stone as a Lonely Charm*, "return to your childhood/& kick out the bottom."

He is especially leary of the bourgeoise mind-traps engineered into his own psychic fiber, and when he writes against the comfortable, instant suburban mystics in "The Suburban prophets," he is consciously blocking out and pushing aside a whole segment of his own origins:

> its easy to quote lao tzu
> when yr wife isnt on the streets
> and you dont have to dodge the
> welfare children
> its an easy cool
> laying on the quiet suburban long grass
> "in tune with the universe."

He is so anti-comfort and pro-suffering, so anti-group and pro-individuality precisely because he sees that group comfort is THE poison that could destroy the clarity of his vision. As he writes in *Tombstone as a Lonely Charm* (Part I), about someone who did allow himself to become part of the bourgeoise mind-central comfort machine:

> i have nothing to say
> if you turn away
> they made a machine
> of/yr mind—once—

```
contained infinite doors
who let them be closed one by one
        not—i—
     have nothing
        to say
        to you
     wont listen-
     turn away.
```

Levy sees even mysticism itself as a kind of trap, a mask to hide behind and obscure the REAL self. He is afraid that if he becomes too much of a "professional mystic," he won't reach, won't touch reality, *out there*—the hard, irritating, suppressive reality that he doesn't want to reject but to understand, comment on, dissect. In *The North American Book of the Dead* (Part IV), Levy writes: "OH! all this tranquility/what the fuck good is it/you can have my buddha nature for a juicy steak & a joint."

In his most widely prophetic and visionary political poems like *Cleveland: The Rectal Eye Vision,* "Beret," and *The Egyptian Stroboscope,* Levy's view of American materialism contrasted with the "spirituality" of other cultures (especially the Egyptian, which has a special fascination for him), while is some ways tangential to the Beat (Ginsberg especially) vision of the U.S., is much more energy-charged, hallucinatory, "psychedelic:"

```
. . . . Cistern of Re . . . foreskin of Tem . . .
crabs of Osiris-Semen of Ra . . . Kotex of
TA-URT . . . used kitty litter of LEMAR-RA . . .
diaper rash of Hep, Taumutaf, Amset and
Qubhsenuf . . . . the testicles of Theth . . . .
(The Egyptian Stroboscope, #6)
```

In a long poem "For Lama Ginsberg," Levy acknowledges a link with Ginsberg, whose *Howl* might really be the starting point for Levy's own later blasting socio-spiritual criticisms ("In my psyche-drama/there is a similarity in our blood"),

but at times Levy is even more effective when he begins to
rear because he has cut further loose from the U.S. world he
is criticizing, is more totally "immersed" in "the other" semi-
historical mystical dreamworld than Ginsberg ever was, *and*
he uses concrete, media-revolution techniques which update
his work and make it more effective to the media-permeated
consciousness.

The reader is bombarded on multiple levels, his with sound
and meaning double-plays, and the page (while still confined
to words, even before moving into pure image collages)
becomes a very effective visual *and* audio medium for slam-
ming home lines:

```
TO RESIST
    ISIS & the
    SAFFRON ROBE
        FROM ROME/ROMA/GALLO/SWISS
        COLONY
        BAYONET IN YUR                        COLON
        YOU ARE BLEEDING                       WINE
WHINE AS YOU DIE                        at the age of 18
YOU have seen the world thru the eyes
of politics
        tic
        tic
        tic (SNAP/BOOM/you are dead. . . . .)
("Beret, A Concrete Poem for the War Monuments.")
```

Levy was always moving "off" the page into pure imagery.
If he had lived or if he'd had any money, he would have probably ended up in experimental film work. Certainly things like
"Beret," with their straining into movement and sound
("politics/tic/tic/tic") all point toward pure visualization.

Even further along in this trajectory are the series of "Visu-
alized Prayers for the American God," in which Levy created
American flags and swastikas and American eagles out of
dollars signs and asterisks. In poems like his "Comment on
the Acid Landscape" (1967), Levy went totally berserk on

the page, projecting disjointed fragments like "is falling, is rising, is falling, is rising, is falling" in erratic patterns mixed in with parentheses and asterisks, dots and number (#) symbols. . . . the visionary here as ascended, the political prophet has been superceded by the pure, floating mystic, a mystic who no longer has to worry about playing or not playing at mysticism, but who definitively and irrevocably IS.

Some idea of Levy's mature trajectory, some inkling of where he was headed for before he committed suicide in 1968, can be garnered from the work he did while in Madison, Wisconsin, in October of 1968.

This work is almost totally visual, printed on cards of varying sizes, issued by Morris Edelson of *Quixote*. Some of the poems, like the "Electric Greek Poems," completely ignore words in terms of their meaning as words, and use them solely in terms of their plastic matrix possibilities. "Home of the Earliest Greek Renaissance Space-Ship Philosophy," for example, one of the "Electric Greek Poems," turns random Greek prose into a kind of "ship," with a kind of "propeller" (exhaust) at one end. The meaning remains fixed in the visualization itself. Greek philosophy is propelling itself through the Renaissance. The expression is essentially non-verbal, immediate, intuitive. Others contained in the same portfolio folder—*7 Concrete Poems*—are more "transition"-concrete, more word-collages with a definite "message" in mind. Like the poem "Napeleon Slept Here" which is developed around a draft notice, peppered with words like "Bazaar," "the Roses of Fire," "The Art-Form of the Future." This is protest-poetry at its most electric, reducing whole paragraphs of "message" to a fragmentary word-shrapnel that cuts through the consciousness with strong, direct impact.

There are others in *7 Concrete Poems* that are more subtle without being any less effective. For example, the "Sun Poem" with the picture of a sun on a card, a PAID stub from the First National Bank in Iowa City, Iowa, superimposed on top of the sun, the words "permanently" and "electric" printed on the card-sides. The Egyptian spirit-sun-world is

contrasted with the dollar, bank-stub image versus sun-god
image . . . again a very effective visualization of a "message."

Among the Madison concrete poetry of Levy there is an
envelope with a cover by T. L. Kryss entitled simply *Quixote,
Vol. 4, No. 6*—d.a. levy, which contains larger "concrete
image" cards that represent some of Levy's wildest, far-out
work. Comic strip characters like Spider Man and Medusa
are flipped down next to girls in black leather, bra ads, pictures of George Washington, cops on empty streets imposing
curfew during riot-times, pictures of Nixon, "nude-cuties,"
medieval saints, fragments of Apollinaire, Egyptian hiere-
glyphics, pictures of bullets, people making love . . . . and
guns and guns and guns. . . . .

In these concrete poems, Levy's vision is apocalyptic, a
phantasmagoric, hallucinatory vision of U.S. society spinning
around in agonizing confusion toward a final, imploded annihilation. Linear, implicit, word-confined Levy here leaps out
into total immediacy, and Levy's worldview comes clear: he is
surrounded by a pornographically sadistic, war-and supres-
sion-oriented society without any redeeming spirituality.
"Pigs versus peace . . . . more fun . . . . with your guns, to
get at the heart of experience . . . . yer thru, creep, with this
punch it's all over . . . . exiles of time . . . . the void . . .
trained at the university ROTC . . . . H-Bomb! your mind
library . . . .," these are the phrases that float across the
surfaces of Levy's collage-mind, and perhaps they are the key
to his own eventual self-destruction.

The pressure had become overwhelming. There was nothing else BUT violence, repression, barbed wire, guns, mind-
control. There was only one more "out"—himself.

"Because there is nothing else to do, Selene and i mount my
white horse that eats chocolate and we ride bareback on the
beach at Coney Island." This fragment from the destroyed
journal, included in ukanhavyrfuckincitibak, is Levy escaping
into a Mire-like landscape of benign ingenuousness. But by
1968 that door into wonderland was also closed, and Levy was

soaked in the blood of the hysterical contemporary purge . . .
or not even "purge," rather indifference:

> you can watch the ones who
> didn't move fast enough
> they are dying
> & they are called Poets
> people used to be afraid of poets
> now they don't listen anymore
> so everything is all right (?)
> (from *Suburban Monastery Death Poem*)

Here Levy, viewing the contemporary scene from the vantage point of the perennial, primordial poet, overviews the
entire relation of the arts to U.S. society, with penetrating
clairvoyance. There are no more Jeremiahs, and the poet as
prophet-visionary has been replaced by the mass media.

Levy is punishingly aware of the fact that poetry has been
replaced by the tube and transister, precisely because tube-
transister communication has so much more impact than
tradition poetry. As he says in *Prose: On Poetry in the Wholesale Education System:*

> i don't know
> poetry seemed like such
> a good idea
> a way to communicate
> pretty pictures
> or to see things that exist
> now. But the people want blood . . .
> the people want blood & guts
> like it is on television
> & in the newspapers—

Levy's concrete/collage poems, his multiple meaning
sound-poems . . . all his experimental work that was straining off the page toward a more complete audio-visual expression, was the last agonizing push inside himself toward

becoming part of the media revolution. Only he didn't make it, couldn't bridge the gap. "I want to eat the television," he writes in the *Suburban Monastery Death Poem,* "becoming the tube/doesn't satisfy the hungry animals inside me/i cant communicate with the damned thing."
The sad irony is that Levy actually rebelled against the very media-energies that he was trying to generate on his own. He was trying to create his own mobile-page television, get the page itself to speak . . . . instead of recognizing that subconsciously he was a media-revolution poet, moving inexorably toward total sight-sound expression.

At the same time, however, on a practical plane, Levy was giving a realistic appraisal of the possibilities of poet-directed media when he wrote: ". . . it hurts/something inside you/when you feel/ like a beggar in an/affluent society . . . ." *(On Poetry in the Wholesale Education & Culture System).* In spite of Levy's deep subconscious need to splice himself onto the media-energies, what chance, really, did he or any other poet have to manipulate media (affluence) toward poetic (beggar) ends?

Another of Levy's last works, *Zen Concrete,* published in October of 1968, is a perfect example of the kind of financial-artistic *cul de sac* that Levy had moved into toward the end of his life. There is a picture of Levy on the cover: emaciated, beat, eyes filled with a mixture of terror and weariness. The word "concrete" is almost fitted in on the bottom of the page, but the cover designer, M. J. Roach, couldn't fit the "te" in so he added them at the top of the page. Inside on the first page is a note from Levy to "Bill" about the book itself, reproduced in his original scrawl, and the book itself is for the most part page after page of blurred lines with a title of a series of lines here and there appearing clear and clean. You could almost think that the effect was intended if some paragraphs didn't come through whole—which they do, Like:

. . . . By Daily Practicing when prana is in
there is no cess at ion devours time of TATTVAJNANA

the Subtle SUSHUMNA is beth (the destruct) ioni-

zation
of the "key" closing her mouth SHE the mind . . . . etc.

This is certainly Levy at his best, extracting the full richness of implication from language ("cess at ion"), playing on sound-sense extensions and mergings ("(the destruct)ionization"), splicing traditional mystical though on to a contemporary word-matrix.

The tragedy, though, is in the production, the "execution," of the book, and the blurred lines, the non-communication of Levy trying to communicate, is symbolic of the whole breakdown of Levy's connection to the world around him.

Levy, perhaps the greatest poet in the U.S. since Ginsberg, never really made it out of the "underground," and when he killed himself, his death made no noise in "polite" New York literary circles. The underground, being underground, is only aware of itself. It is a giant, creative sensitive conscience that digests and then comments on the U.S. behind the plastic, computerized facade. Only the overground world remains self-contained and cut off from this underground conscience, and it is this severing, this gap, that really destroyed Levy. He was a prophet who had reached such a degree of isolation that his prophecies blurred, twisted, warped, and then stopped.

"Poetry should not be just for poets—the people who make guns do not go hungry," wrote Levy in *On Poetry in the Wholesale Education & Culture System,* slightly envious of that other form of communication which has come so much to the fore recently among young artists—violence. Only Levy, the poet who always stuck by his non-committment to ANY creeds, who maintained his stand of "I'm not advocating anything," could not really subscribe to violence either and so, groupless, even in an increasingly politicized underground, he retired into himself in suicide:

my peer group?

goodbye television
im going back inside my head
(from SUBURBAN MONASTERY DEATH POEM)

Brown Miller

Although Brown Miller at first glance may look like a member of the California (San Francisco-Sacramento) School of poets, celebrating life and joy and trying to return to ingenuous, direct, simplified expression, he isn't. He has been published by The Runcible Spoon (D. r. Wagner) and Open Skull Press (Doug Blazek), but in many respects his work is very different from either that of Wagner or Blazek. Blazek himself acknowledges this difference in the "Introduction" of *Fertilized Brains* (1968) when he writes about Miller: "HIS poems are monsters—they are not like my poems or your poems. . . ."

First of all, Miller does not participate in either the meat-school mystique of a Blazek or in the return-to-childhood mystique of a Wagner, because his roots are in an earlier, "straighter" tradition, a twisted, inverted, Calvinistic Catholicism. He is really closer to Donne or Pascal than Blazek's neo-Naturalism or Wagner's neo-transcendentalism. When you meet him he seems to be "one of the guys," moustached, affable, easy to talk to, a good listener, a good contributer to a good conversation but he isn't "one of the guys" at all, but hides under his protective facade a frightening God- and sin-centered vision of the world that for the most part has gone out in twentieth century North America . . . . especially in California.

The basis for this interpretation of Miller's work can be found in a mimeographed poem-cycle that he sent me a few

25

months ago called *On the Banks Of the* I Ching, *A Reversible Cycle of Poems.* In most of Miller's published work the orthodox sin-redemption dichotomy is implied, but here in *On the Banks of the* I Ching the references are quite explicit.

Sex is evil, something filthy and vile:

> Oh God, there's a
> serpent in your pants!
> ("Soul Bed")

Sin is necessary to salvation:

> Help me find some
> meaningful sin
> or I'll never
> be saved.
> ("Sculptor & Nympth")

Miller himself is damned:

> My lover gave me a
> snake for Christmas . . . .
> I asked her why.
> To watch it die . . . and her
> innocent laughing
> caught me in a
> shining cage of ice
> where I could finally
> see
> that my skin was
> falling.
> ("Gift Magic")

Miller's confessor is a whiskey priest "(who lately/drinks for three)." ("Sacrament")

Miller's Christianity, of course, is twisted. It is harsh, puritannical, Jansanistic and views man as basically depraved, unworthy of salvation, something disgusting, unhealthy, despicable. And because of this basically "sick" nature, everything that man does is ugly, evil, warped. As Miller says in another poem which I have in mimeo:

> we strangle our lives to live
> with the disease we call love.
> ("I Do Not Understand This Extermination You Have
> Performed In Me.")

Apart from the *On the Banks of the* I Ching cycle perhaps the single most self-revealing poem that Miller ever wrote is "I Have Been Given These Words." It is more than a wasteland poem, it is a poem conceived and developed in a hell of total self-deprecation and self-contempt. We are born guilty, just because we are ourselves (". . . we breathe in ruts,/guilt-weary beneath a curse") and all our most idealistic activity parodies Christ's Last Supper, which ends, not in crucifixion, but something even more vile, nakedness, an exposure to the full corruption of our own inner selves:

> Now we perform
> obscure suppers: break bread,
> swallow the yellow wine,
> watch the jerking zombies
> in their black mass.
> Finally we sink into nudity.

For the most part straightforeward and traditional (with some happy exceptions), Miller's distinctiveness lies in the re-exploration of already abandoned world-views. The application of the doctrine of Original Sin (original depravity) to the contemporary scene, in Brown's hands takes on a meaningful significance. The mystique of depravity, perhaps more than any contemporary system, "fits" our world, and Brown's crooked, hell-fire approach has a special piquancy and meaningfulness that many of his more optimistic, less traditional peers lack.

In *Fertilized Brains,* perhaps Miller's single most powerful work, the impact of his vision is especially poignant where in a poem like "Flesh Poem" he relates an experience like the search for a free unhampered love-sex life to the rigidity of traditional values:

                    The powerful
                uterine muscle, like an
                aged cask in dark ground,
              has reached a delicate violence,
          and I see it strain
                        all alone
              to unconsciously
                                    spew
          a prayer
                        of atheism.

The line "she disguises her fear with motion" cuts through multiple layers of the self-deception of a generation which refuses to acknowledge any kinship with a past, dead, "square" world, and stresses the generation gap in order to leave behind as far as possible the guilt which continues to plague it.

Miller's contemporaries, under their love-generation mask, have still been raised in families tied to strict square values, and the sex-liberation impulse viewed as a reaction against the too-obviously-present past, is a "prayer of atheism" —which is, as he notes, "unconscious." By bringing to the surface the whole structure of traditional values and contrasting these values with the actual world around him, he crystallizes the invisible, concretizes the subconscious, brings into play a traditional dimension operative within his generation that they are unaware of, and which they want to remain unaware of.

Sex, for Miller, instead of being the usual panacea that it is for so many of his contemporaries, is infused with a primordial sense of horror and disgust. One of his basic tenents, after all, is that the flesh is evil, and evil must proceed from evil. Nowhere is this more vividly portrayed than in another poem from *Fertilized Brains,* "Nuptial Funeral," where in a man suffering from complications after a circumcision, is taunted by a nurse and destroyed in a final act of grotesquely combined sex and self-destruction:

> then goes into her act of strip & flaunt,
> shewing ghostly black whisps,
> yes the dirtiness of it all
> was part of his downfall,
> but the very fact that he knew
> it would kill him
> is what really sprung the lock open
> and for a fierce terrified consolation,
> in his last blood-spurting convulsions,
> he rapes the laughing wench,
> pumping reddened sperm,
> knowing it will fertilize her whole guts,
> grinning madly and dying glad.

"The dirtiness of it all/was part of his downfall . . ." Here Miller the guilt-harassed Puritan extends out his view of man's depravity to dwell on the inevitable linking together of death and sex.

"Death," he writes in *The World Is Coming* ("Air That Closes, Freezes"), *"is the final physical act,"* and a Calvinistic preoccupation with death, decay, dying, is infused throughout all of Miller's work. He is a Calvinist stripped even of the possibility of "election," damned to condemnation in this world, hung on the cross of existential time, unable to move, much less get down. For him the world is trapped in a hopeless spiral of entropy: "What seems to bloom is actually decaying . . ." ("One More Dance Again," *The World Is Coming*). Time is inevitable, irrevocably running down carrying him along with it to a final step: "of time/spiral decaying/take me." (9, *33 Phases of the Fatal Stroboscope*). His whole development, his whole salvation, lies in a contrasting back into himself, passing the macroscopic limits of

awareness, moving into the limits of the subliminal and sub-conscious: ". . . my pathways of perceiving/are my own again,/wings of blood migrating/in toward the centers, out past all limits." ("The Poet as Salesman," in *Fertilized Brains*) He can never move beyond the limits of his decay-oriented vision ("the smell of dead blood under me/heat of too much space above me"), but is trapped in a world whose beginnings and ends are dipped in death: "I am on the bridge of corpses/kingdom my kingdom!" ("I Am on the Bridge of Corpses," *The World Is Coming*).

This death-decay orientation of Miller's emotions is geneti-cally linked with a distaff and morbid view of Christianity, but there is also a strong morbid familial element which con-tributes to his negative bent. His book, *Auto-Psies and Family Ghosts,* (1968) is subtitled "A Documentary on Word Poi-soning," which, within the context of the book's thematic material, links together his macabre family life and the macabre flavor of much of his work.

His father emerges as a time-and work-obsessed punisher. In *33 Phases of the Fatal Stroboscope,* Miller characterizes his father in terms of his having eaten "a clock at a very early age/& the dogs have been/his weapon against me," (12) and in *Auto-Psies and Family Ghosts* he expands on this portrait and links his father with his own strong sense of guilt:

> in our first house
> we were concerned with
> cockroaches and father said
> I should nibble them
> from the walls
> at night
> because I was being punished
> he said for something he knew
> I would do sooner or later
> an act which was
> a sin and very unclean.

His father twisted him toward an oral disgust-masochism

(nibbling coakroaches) and then overshadowed his entire life
with a kind of Original Sin—which he would inevitably com-
mit, and which would cloud and dirty his entire life ("a sin
and very unclean"). Here Miller's individual will is dominated
by a cosmic curse, an inevitable need for "uncleaness" (sin) in
the universe. Miller is trapped.

His teeth rot, he complains to his mother about having to
eat cockroaches and his mother screams out "I've been in the
grave/these past three years/since you killed me when/you
were six years old." His father tries to give him a lesson in
drowning in the kitchen sink—without touching him "(which
he didn't want to do)"—and Miller gets stuck in the drain and
his stepmother tries to suck him out ("the up-down rhythm")
only fails. If there'd been a garbage disposal, he asks himself,
"would she have set its grinding blades in motion and would I
have been flushed into the sewer in tiny shreds and out to
sea?"

This symbolically rich grotesquerie expands and develops
and he returns obsessively to the theme of his mother. She had
been paralyzed, wet the bed, was brought to the hospital, and
ten days later died, her death, her manner of dying, filtering
into and poisoning Miller's whole life. As he puts it:

> my mother has infected
> my bones, crying
> at the marrow, speaking
> to some dusty wandering
> mirrors that I once lost
> in there deep somewhere. . . .

Not only did his mother die grotesquely, but his time-and
guilt-obsessed father wished her dead—"my father pissed
minutes/like poisoned darts/& begged her/to stay dead." (*33
Phases of the Fatal Stroboscope,* 20)—and then married a
woman whose grey, stringent, punishing vision of the world
matched his own. Strong and forcefully exaggerated in his
imagery, Miller characterizes his sister as a kind of awkward

extension of his father's worldview ("my sister had her
stomach/sewn up right in front of her/boy friend so he would
know/she was faithful"), and then pin-points down his stepmother's religious bents and sets them off against a psychological landscape of sex and emasculation:

> . . . . our
> step-mother (who is sometimes
> present) flew into a heated
> cage battering her gray head
> because she had been raised
> a strict presbyterian and
> therefore thought the whole
> scene was obscene,
> whereupon I made my exit
> walking . . . . . to
> the city dump . . . . and
> . . . . began digging in the garbage
> searching for discarded girlie magazines . . . .
> . . . . . . descending
> to plant (them) in my father's
> nightstand where my step-mother
> will castrate him
> for good.

Miller tops off this series of portraits of family ghosts with
a portrait of his wife. His past extends into his present, cor-
rupting and twisting it, disallowing any time of "normal"
relationship to ever develop, necessarily distorting all sex-love
relationships into diseased, deformed parodies. Instead of
escaping from his childhood, Miller allows his childhood to
dominate his entire life:

> . . . . . wanting to
> forget I'd ever kissed her,
> knowing the ruthless texture of
> her body, which trapped me in
> a nightmare of the time
> I sprawled above her small frame

and held into places of hers
that were shrouded in ice
and I turned away, wishing I
had learned how to cry,
submitting to the
avalanche of nausea.

Perhaps the key phrase here is "avalanche of nausea."
Love, sex, tenderness, flesh all trigger the avalanche of nausea. Miller is trapped and isolated in nausea and nausea gives
form and dimension to his entire vision of reality. Miller
never steps out of nausea, never experiences one moment of
isolated joy, happiness, fulfillment, apart from and independent of nausea.

Beginning with flesh, family, a warped childhood, Miller's
vision of the nausea-infused world reaches cosmic propor-
tions in his *Whiskeytown Iron Mountain Triptych* (1968).
Part I, "Churn Creek Road," represents a withdrawal and
retreat from the contemporary world back to a decaying,
primitive world in the California mountains, the prototype of
the world after the Fall:

. . . a valley of a-
mazed mazes of pale trees
with mystic labor & sweat
tearing up the minerals
from the road's spine
where old fat indian men
their maps long ago decayed
limp into the pacheco store
where money haunts the sky
& the road curves softly
toward empty fields of
yellow grass turned into
death's sister by the sun.

In a morbidly brilliant gnostic twist on "traditional" the-
ology, Miller sees not the devil, but god (specifically Christ)

as the cause of this world's broken decay. The devil has been destroyed, the snake split open by a Mexican girl's (the "Virgin") powered mower ("her . . . mower splitting it in half/lengthwise/turning it inside out/stripping it of its evil/& saving its red soul to dry/serpent black in the bright"), and now the world has been left to operate within the carefully directed mechanisms of the divine.

In Part II, the fish hatchery, a prototype of all life, illustrates Miller's attitude toward life in its inception, its essence. The fish are born "squirming" in a "stink of life." Life from the beginning is ugly, stinking rotten.

This statement on the "essence" of life is followed by a classic portrayal of anti-love, love twisted, burnt, charred, love in which flesh is contaminated and a touch a torture:

> . . . . you touch her
> & yr hand dies among her
> breathings & yr skin burns
> as it plays desperately in
> her hair and it is the color
> or iron mountain's cut side
> like the rust of god's sword.

God's punishment and wrath is given a further twist. It is not a destroying, annihilating wrath, but a wrath that undermines and corrodes. God's sword is not shining, new, strong . . . . but rusted.

Then, confronted with the reality of "iron mountain," which again serves as a type-symbol for the entire earth, Miller makes his farthest-reaching statement concerning man and the universe:

> . . . . when
> the dull blue corpse of earth
> lies with a dry red wound
> our question of Why and How
> are grotesque midgets of ego
> and the whole god-fucked galaxy

is the crucifix on which
our planet grinds out
its sterile sacrifice.

Man, Miller is saying, is faced by a dead earth in a dead universe, is inevitably forced back into meaninglessness. Some god, some demon-Christ has created a meaningless universe and set it spinning in the emptiness of eternal space, and all motion, progress, sacrifice, love, whatever is sterile because it stems from and is contained in this fundamental meaninglessness.

Love, the only solution that Miller presents ANYWHERE is, really, only a temporary and partial solution in terms of his overwhelmingly nihilistic world-view: Even in *Yes We Are Living in this Ocean, a Word Mosaic for Sharon* (1968), love, flesh, the breaking of solitude through sexual intimacy, any solution is ephemeral, fragile, transitory:

this dance is our
      mother, and
the drums our father:
practice my flesh!
oh we dream into
      each other
push out the devils
eat blue stars
live a flaming
      holiday of skin
invent movements
your mouth is
      revealed at last
can i worship in it?

yes we are wind
from this eye,
ocean's lung,
green dance.

Love ("this dance") here becomes a kind of exorcism, freeing Miller from his familial past, converting his gnostic

despair in the sterility of the world into a "flaming holiday of skin."
But even here the holiday "flames," burns, tortures. And, instead of lasting, it becomes wind, a temporary, seasonal outburst, all life, even the life of love, merely a breath of the *"ocean's lung."*
Miller, then, remains the Calvinist, the sin-scorched, the tortured, the pessimist, at the opposite pole from Hippie optimism, not really a member of the Blazek-Richmond-Bukowski "Meat School," at the same time kindred to the Meat Poets in his urgent need to confront and grapple with the totality of his own reality-vision. Miller's popularity among his contemporaries, his acceptance by as tough and unyielding a critic as Blazek, stems from the fact that Miller's sin- and corruption-soaked worldview is so close to the wave of Neo-Naturalism supported by Blazek, which attempts to drill through conventionalities (and conventional poetry) into an expression of life stripped to the raw, essential, "real." As Blazek puts it in a letter to Miller reprinted in *Life in a Common Gun:*

> . . . . in all of this experimentation & art
> you have not lost touch w/the earth, w/the
> soil, w/biology—you have retained a
> non-bullshit openminded attitude towards
> life—yr writing becomes an extension of yr
> humanness not a dichotomy.

Then, too, Blazek's and Richmond's and Bukowski's OWN origins are puritannical, sin-dyed, conscience-soaked, and Miller's agonized expression of reality touches their own most conservative, traditional past.
Miller's work, though, for all its squareness and weight of tradition both in content and execution, is hip because it is "different." In the midst of a brave new world of flower and love children, Miller has had the audacity to be true to his own origins and write about his own not-too-private world of thorns and hate.

Dick Higgins: Neo-Dadaist

In 1917 in Zurich, Switzerland, a new artistic movement called "DADA" began which in a sense set the "tone" for most avant-garde twentieth century art. Dada was an "anti-art" movement—anti-logic, anti-sense, anti-order, anti-continuity. It wanted to break the whole of western artistic and philosophical tradition into bits and pieces, destroy the past, annihilate the very metaphysical foundations of western civilization.

Dada was the most radical extension of an essential split between "high" and "low" culture. The Viennese expressionist-atonalist musicians like Webern, Alban Berg and Schoenberg are indicative of the form this split was taking. The atonalists definitely "smashed" the traditional western tonal system and substituted their own in its place, creating a music that was not popular, not understood, certainly not enjoyed. Perhaps the only work done by the atonalists that has reached any wide audience is Berg's highly dramatic opera "Wozzeck"—for the rest, atonalism has retained only a small, esoteric group of followers. At the same time tonal music has continued to be produced (Ricard Strauss, Mahler, Prokofieff, etc.) and atonal music has "progressed" into electronic and concrete music (Varese, Stockhausen, etc.). Classical music has split into two camps, the traditionalists and the avantgardists . . . . a split which has been accompanied on the "low culture" level by the development of a massive "pop" music culture: everything from the Beatles and the Rolling Stones to Judy Collins and Buffy St. Marie.

Within these three divisions, High Culture has been characterized by its remoteness, its inaccessability, by the fact it cannot be simply "enjoyed," but must be "studied" to be appreciated, that it has become increasingly incomprehensibel to "outsiders" and has created a small elite of understanding "faithful." Low Culture, on the other hand, although within an understandable tradition, has lost ground to Pop Culture—and the folk singers and rock and roll artists have all but replaced serious composers like Samuel Barber or Roy Harris. Pop Culture, simple, straightforeward, always adapted to contemporary conditions, using the contemporary media as a mass-communication outlet, at the same time that it represents a vulgarization of music as a creative mode, also has become increasingly sophistocated, even, at times, "difficult." African and Hindu rhythms and instruments have been introduced, a whole hallucenogenic coloring of electronic instruments combined with light shows, has produced a massive audience which is capable of responding—as it did at a recent Monterrey Jazz Festival—to the best of Hindu classical artists: Ravi Shankar. In other words, both High and Pop culture are "demanding" and "complex," whereas Low Culture is neither.

The situation in music has been duplicated in most of the other arts. In the theater, the nineteenth century "well-made" play has moved through the Theater of the Absurd and Happenings into Anti-Theater (High Culture) while the broadway musical and "straight" plays continue on as if Ionesco and Beckett never had existed. There is at least one notable case of a playwright in the U.S. who began as an exponent of High Culture and has slowly moved down to Low Culture: Albee. At the same time the movies represent a classic example of the full development of an alternative Pop Culture—a theatrical form totally adapted to the electronic world, at the same time becoming increasingly "demanding" and "complex" without becoming "esoteric." Television, being almost a totally commercial medium cannot really as yet be taken seriously in terms of any of these three cultural divisions.

In literature since Dada and Surrealism there has been an accelerating push toward complete esotericism and obscurantism. "High Culture" for a long time has ignored "the public," and poetry in the High Culture camp has become a game of an elite in-group. At the same time "Low Culture" has been supported by the academy and a huge body of traditional, dull, *deja vu* poetry has been produced which is right in line with Edgar Lee Masters and Robert Frost. The younger poets, often also folk-singers or movie-makers have tried to create a Pop Culture Poetry that fastens on to the "media" and swings with an electronic beat. I remember Andy Clausen at the 1968 COSMEP Conference in Berkeley reading like a wildman a poem that sung and swung like Kerouac, Ginsberg and King Kong, taking his clothes off until he was stripped down naked, the whole audience stamping their feet and screaming, a girl in the back taking off her clothes in sympathetic protest . . . . poetry had become "Pop," it became a happening, street theater, guerilla action.

High Culture in literature, of course, has always had a much bigger audience in Europe than in the U.S. Dada and surrealism were essentially European movements, atonalism never really caught on in the U.S. the way it did in Europe . . . . and in spite of Milton Babbitt's experiments in electronic music, the U.S. didn't really have a high-culture priest until John Cage came along.

The alienation, the suffocating sense of traditionalism, the collapse of whole value systems, the disenchantment with a whole cultural mystique that produced Dadaism and Surrealism and Expressionism in Europe, never really took hold in the U.S. in the twenties and thirties—even the forties. U.S. culture was too pliable and elastic to need a reaction as radical as Dada in order to break it down. It didn't have to break, but could bend. Besides, traditional U.S. psychic isolationism did not allow the U.S. artist to become totally involved with

the European existentialist breakdown of western values. The
essential "horror" of existence—Satre's "nausea"—was
always European, something "over there," somehow divorced
and detached from U.S. psychic life.

Dick Higgins is one the the very few High Culture poets in
the U.S. Perhaps the only justification for classifying himself
as "underground" at all is that he's not really accepted by
the "overground" (Low Culture) either . . . and because he
himself does make an effort to maintain close contact with
the underground world. He doesn't even LOOK underground though and when dropped down into the midst of a
gathering of the underground clan, like at the COSMEP
Conference in Ann Arbor in June of 1969, his white shirts
and suits and ties, in the midst of sweatshirts and sport
shirts, buckskins and African prints, are very conspicuous.

Also, he is very little understood by the rest of the Underground. At the 1969 COSMEP Conference he showed two
films, one about his two children in summertime rural Vermont, the other about a rural hatchet-killing. . . . also set
in Vermont. No one seemed to quite know whether the
corney murder film or the corney home-movie-like film
about his kids were to be taken seriously or not, until
Higgins gave them the clue by laughing. It was New York
humor, "camp," "in," very sophisticated-taking the cornball
and converting it into high satire.

This is the way Higgins wants most of his work to be taken,
never seriously, in spite of a deceptively serious facade, in
spite of complicated methodology and an impressive aura of
critical terminology—but as satire at its most attenuated and
sensitive limit.

As head of Something Else Press in New York he has been
THE prime mover in introducing European avant-garde literature (especially poetry) into the U.S., and this European
link is really the key to Higgins' alienation from the rest of
the American underground scene. The undergrounders are—
I'm thinking of Levy, Blazek, Krech—very self-conscious
prophets. They see themselves very much in terms of the

Shelleyan "seer-visionary" function. And even those non-preacher poets like Sharon Asselin who merely capture an evanescent glint and spark of light in their works, without the slightest social or philosophical "purpose," still feel the need to communicate some logical, consistent, meaningful experience:

> i return with lips still wet
> from yr pulse, press them
> against yr brow for judgement,
> bury them in yr hair like two thieves
> who have stolen life
> at yr fountain.
> (Sharon Asselin, from *Return to Barth*)

Higgins' work, on the contrary, is purposefully anti-logical, anti-meaning, in fact the subversion of the entire basic western value system.

Take, for example, his *A Book About Love & War & Death*. Subjectwise, he tells us in the preface, he wanted to base the work on things that were "meaningful" to him:

> . . . . for a focus I wanted to list the things that meant the most to me. In the Spring of 1960 my brother Mark left Dr. Schweitzer's hospital, where he had been an assistant, and went to the Congo, where independence was followed by civil war. Roughly simultaneous to this I was married in New York. During the Summer Mark was killed, because he was a white man. The three events became very deeply connected in my mind, and so I chose love and war and death as my touchstones. . . . .

The work itself, though, is not only *not* meaningful emotionally or intellectually, but has been purposefully turned into a topsy-turveydom of "smart," smug gibberish.

In the preface to Cantos 2 and 3 of *A Book About Love & War & Death* (1969) Higgins explains his methodology of composition as a variation on the application of "chance and logical test structures to language" along the lines of similar work by Jackson Mac Low. He began with a 202 page English-Indonesian dictionary and three dice:

> . . . . each die has six sides, so there were 6 × 6 × 6, or 216 possible numbers. I let each throwing reference a page number, and used the first unused word on that page in a subject list. This gave me a fourteen pages (up to the 216 pages needed) of Bahasa Indonesia . . . . As each word was used, it was crossed off. In this way I figured I would slowly use up most of the common words in English, and spice up the inevitably Latinate tone of such a proceding with the Indonesian materials.

Essentially, then, Higgins began with series of word lists, and the only conscious "control" or "manipulation" of these lists was in the manner that he put them together:

> . . . I began the BOOK, taking lists of words and structuring them into sentences, either lyrical or grammatical, according to rules which were consistent, section by section, but not section to section. At the start of some sections I would think, let's have a psalm, and I'd think my acts of writing in terms of a psalm. Or let's do straight prose, and I'd do it.

Using a chance-determined content, then, Higgins merely concentrates on nuance and "tone," and arrives at a product that not only seems completely without any relation to love and war and death, but which is totally inconsistent and self-cancelling even within itself:

> Copper is to roast a nobleman.
> When, as a diebetic presses and cites a random aspal, when dissension is all wrapped up and outstanding, an infinite crate taken as an adhesion is an advantage . . . .
> No aircraftsman can hiss.
> Neither can there reign any symptom. . . . .

In 1966 Higgins' Something Else Press published a pamphlet by George Brecht entitled *Chance-Imagery* in which the whole history of chance and randomness is laid out.

Dada, of course, is the starting point, but Brecht brings in everything from game and probability theory to Heisenberg's principle of indeterminacy, and concludes that man is a random cosmos, that "chance . . . [is] an underlying principle of our world-view." In terms of the enlarging, liberating influence of chance on art, Brecht concludes that only through chance can man liberate himself from a basically false (logical) world view and move into a grasp of the real world exterior to the deceptive structuring of the human mind:

> Science tells us that the universe is what we conceive it to be, and chance enables us to determine what we conceive it to be (for the conception is only partly conscious). The receptacle of forms available to the artist thus becomes open-ended, and eventually embraces all of nature, for the recognition of significant form becomes limited only by the observer's self. It must be obvious too that the infinite range of application of these methods is compounded when the matter of materials . . . . is also considered, and we fall short of the infinite expansion of the human spirit for which we are searching, when we recognize only images which are artifacts. We are capable of more than that.

Very much anti-artifact, in *A Book About Love & War & Death,* Higgins is really more observer than "artificer," more passive onlooker than creator. Subordinating his brother's death, his own marriage, his own personal feelings to a chance procedure involving three dice and a dictionary, Higgins allows a world to come into being next to, apart from, independent of his own inner, subjective world of emotions and needs.

In spite of a great variety of themes and techniques found throughout Higgins' work—with actually very little of it based on the theories of chance—there is a certain similarity of "tone" in everything that Higgins has done. Everything he does is in one way or other a "novelty," a "departure," a "freakshow," a "prodigy."

In an essay on "Structural Researches" contained in *FOEWE&OMBWHNW* (Freaked Out Electronic Wizards & Others Marvelous Bartenders Who Have No Wings), Higgins rather strongly attacks the "formalism" of much modern art for subordinating the free-play of affective and creative elements to a pre-determined formal structure:

> . . . I would like to assert that work which allows either the pole of novelty or of tradition in its formal considerations to dominate the actual form the work will ultimately assume is utterly unrealistic and irrelevant. Structural innovation cannot in my opinion derive from *a priori* considerations, oriented towards tradition or novelty, but is absolutely without exception a concomitant of any work that is open to the new rhetoric of a dialectic between structure and meaning and which is at all sensitive to its own needs in its realization.

The problem of imposing *a priori* forms on art is very intimately related to Higgins' own practice of imposing an *a priori* "mode of operations" based on novelty. The need to be "novel," to be "avant-garde," to always be "different" is just as confining a role as the need to impose any form, either novel or traditional, on a given work of art. Form may vary, but the working area of novelty in itself is very limiting. And the increasing egotericism imposed by the strictures of High Culture eliminate any kind of "simple" (Low or Pop Culture) statement, any unrefined (reworked) sentiment, any already-seen structure, really any gut empathy or identification between work and audience. Form eventually completely dominates content and the work of art itself becomes solely a game of methodology.

This is true even in works designed specifically for "participation," in which the work is left open-ended and flexible. A good example of this kind of methodological game (similar to

A Book About Love & War & Death not in the kind of but concentration on methodology) is Higgins' *The Tart, or Miss America.* Here methodology reigns supreme. There are "between three and eleven regular performers and one special performer" required. The characters (Higgins calls them "personae") that must be portrayed are: the young man, Mr. Miller and the tart. Other characters can be introduced are the old man, the prophet, the butchers, the doctors, the drinking man, the chemist, the yogi, the steelworkers, and the electricians.

The characters are given 36 "situations" (such as "A very large object is brought in or removed," or "A postage stamp is attached to something or somebody") and 30 "speeches" (such as "Behold the sea, saith the Lord," or "What would loving him be like, asks the tart") and Higgins carefully sets down an elaborate set of ground-rules:

> Each performer now lists twenty-two stage actions of his own devising such that no action requires the use of a particular prop or the presence of a particular person on the stage. To this list he adds "Exit" ten times and "Entrance" four times. This list of action is now assigned to the thirty-six situations given below at random, with any number of actions assigned to any of the situations. In the case where there is more than one action for a given situation, the performer now determines whether he will perform all the actions or choose among them. Exit and entrance action are always followed.

> Next the performer assigns all the thirty speeches given below to situations, with the option of assigning a speech to more than one situation but never of assigning more than one speech to a given situation. The performers now may begin to rehearse together. . . . . .

The result, although not as fanatically random as the Indonesian dictionary technique used to construct *A Book*

About Love & War & Death, is calculated to destroy any
sequential narrative and its inevitable product, empathy: "As
it has no psychological empathy, THE TART does not permit
the audience to view it as a play or ballet." Instead the audience is expected to sympathize, not with the "characters" but
the "performers" themselves in a kind of grotesque extension
of Pirandello's *Six Characters In Search of an Author.*

In his preface to *The Tart* Higgins insists that he is interested in emphasizing the "subject matter by eliminating narrative" and throughout the "speeches" there *is* a kind of
social-message overtone:

> Light and electricity, say the electricians.
>
> But what can I do about it, ask the electricians.
>
> The steelworkers say no. No, say the steelworkers.
> (No. No.)

And if no message gets through and there is no sympathiz-
ing with the "performers in their social contexts," Higgins
has also provided an answer for that: "It was not successful;
neither was it intended to be." The *real* intention remains
experimentation for the sake of experimentation, novelty for
the sake of novelty, an application of "collage to theatre," the
expression of Higgins, the musician, "in rebellion against
. . . . his medium."

Trying to understand Higgins as basically a musician out of
water in drama *or* poetry, is very fruitful. In his introduction
to "Graphic," an article published in the *Tulane Drama
Review* in the winter of 1965, Higgins reveals the source of
many of the techniques he applies to literature as basically
musical:

> Experimental music has frequently used extraordinary
> notations. Stockhausen, Graettinger, and Cage have
> found notations which expand musical vocabularies. So
> I started out with drawn notations such as, "The Higher
> up on this page this line goes, reading from left to right,

the louder you speak. Where there are two lines to be
read vertically you choose." What I did not specify
was what was to be said. I thought people would quote
the newspapers.

Higgins, the musician, then, isn't really interested in meaning but in tone, timbre, line, movement. Meaning is a super-
fluous "extra," added to an art that is essentially non-verbally
meaningful.

Non-verbal meaning, not dependent on the transmission of
concepts as such, is much more structured "in itself," much
more "formal" (formcentric), than verbal meaning, and if
we consider the totality of Higgins' work we see that what
he essentially is is a displaced musician lost in a world of
words. *A Book About Love & War & Death* is
essentially random, chance "word-music,"—and so is
most of Higgins' work. Very seldom does he stray into
coherence, sequence, "verbal meaning."

Perhaps the high point of Higgins' use of words, non-
cognitionally as "pure music" is in his plays *Saint Joan at
Beaurevoir* (contained in *FOEW&OMBWHNW*). Like *A
Book About Love & War & Death, Saint Joan at Beaurevoir* is based on "randomness":

> The durations of scenes, actions and sounds and the
> sequences of events are all derived by chance structures
> through the use of such notations as the one reproduced
> in John Cage's book *Notations.*

Words are to a great extent as "purely musical constella-
tions of phoenemes" and in the preface a list of 75 phonemes
is included that describes exactly how the various sounds
should be pronounced: "oy-long "oy" as in "joy," k-"k" as in
"kale," etc. People shake their heads, St. Joan bends "side-
ways at the waist, back to the audience, back and forth six or
seven times," someone says (fortissimo) "Cans are in
sequence, $4.70," people comb their hair, fill coffee pots, play
chess, write letters, all accompanied by music "made by

assembling electrical flashers and cube taps which turn on and off, at random, such noise-producing electrical objects as vacuum cleaners, hair dryers, drills, sirens, tape recorders, radios, door chimes, buzzers, etc." The characters, except for St. Joan, really have nothing to do with St. Joan, and include Napoleon, Piers Ploughman, Diogenes the Cynic, Santa Claus, P. T. Barnum, Chou En-lai, Martha Washington, Madame Curie, Jack Sprat's Wife, Florence Nightingdale and Saint Margaret of Hungary. When Saint Joan does talk her speeches come out:

> Seteem its hall niorgiz niz, and an unat!,

or

> Kszrd dq' ovr, yjr aobomh ujrsyrt, 641 sbrmir
> pg yjr szrtovad, mre uptl 22, mu . . . .

The whole work has nothing to do with literature as such, but is an exercise in form emptied of any but strictly formal meaning.

This concentration on "pure form" is even more highly developed in Higgins' "Design Plays" in which choreography is the single most important element. In his pamphlet *Towards the 1970's* (1969), Higgins acknowledges the importance of contemporary dancers like Yvonne Rainer, Judith Dunn and Trisha Brown, and shows himself very much absorbed by the idea of pure ballet form, In his "Design Plays," Higgins tries his own hand at this kind of basic, essential, core form . . . . totally divorced from any meaning beyond itself. The entire emphasis here is "on what happens, on how it happens, and on the relationships which arise from the material."

There are nine numbered performers. The costumes are in black and white or black and off-white. Slides are used along with five musical fragments, "preferably electronic." The plays themselves are identified by an *a* through *e* lettering system and are "intermixed" through a complicated system of cueing so that a vastly complex system of interwoven forms is created. Some idea of the edge-of-chaos effect Higgins is trying to achieve can be gotten from the stage directions that preface the plays. Starting with the music fragments, Higgins writes:

> . . . . Each fragment is labeled with a letter from *a* to *e*. When it is played, all the performers perform the corresponding play, combining the designated play with whatever slide or other situation is onstage when the music is recognized. Any performer who is not included in the play designated by the music goes offstage, but continues to regard any cues he receives as belonging to the play he was performing before the music cue took place. At his next entrance, he enters. Any person who is in the play designated by the music, but who was not onstage when the music began, enters at once and performs from whatever cue is taking place. . . . . .

> Performers take their cues onstage by checking the color being projected on them at each new side. A quick glance at the slide projector will suffice to indicate what color is falling on the performer's head. If the color situation is one for which the performer has a cue in the play he is performing, he responds by performing his action efficiently and imaginatively without losing his dignity. It is hoped that each performer will respond to the freedom implicit in the cuing system by allowing his better instincts to move him. . . .

In practice this cuing system produces a fascinating choreographic richness which never really emerges exactly the same during two consecutive performances.

Instead of having the play written as most plays are in terms of "play-sequence," Higgins' design plays are written in terms of the "actor-sequence." A typical set of "actor-directions" would be:

> 9 (i.e. the 9th actor)
> in a & b (i.e. in plays a & b)

1b. Slump for two steps, straighten for two steps, slump for two steps, straighten for two steps, etc. when you walk. 2b. In red light say, *mp* "Is found to the dairy, the wash-home or mistress of the house can be. Is found to? Havd burrowed under looked for during is found to the dairy, the mistress of the year." Switch to a. 3a. In amber light, say, "The dairy the wash-house or. If a mole mistress of the. If a mole is found to mistress of the the coming year." etc.

The "sequence" of action is determined by a "density chart" in which the plays are designated from right to left from a–e, and the "situations" are set up horizontally in terms of colors. For example:

	Plays				
Situations	a	b	c	d	e
I-general	1,4, 7	1,5, 6,9	2,5,	3,5,	3
2-red	1,4, 7	1,3, 5,6, 7,9.	5,6	4	3,8.
3-amber	1,2, 6,7, 8,9	1,5, 7,9	2,8	5	3,7,8

etc.

The result of this sublimely complex nonsense is an intermingling of bodies, sounds, lights, colors, words. . . . a kind of action painting being painted right before the spectator's eyes. The design plays are electronic ballet, aleatic controlled happenings, cybernetic fantasies of essential "form."

Higgins' "Design Plays" illustrate better than any other of his works just how different he is from the rest of the U.S. underground. Higgins' real companions in art aren't the Blazeks and the Levys, the Wagners or the Asselins, but Lynn Lonnidier, the San Diego kookout word-witch, or Lynn's roommate Pauline Olivieros, the electronic musician, Meredith Monk, the new-new-new New York ballerina, John Cage, the mystic madness "electronicist," . . . . or abroad, J. F. Bory, the French word experimentalist, Clemente Padin, the Uruguayan phonic poet, Edvargo Vigo, the Argentinian "comprehensive dadaist."

Perhaps Higgins' work is an arrow pointing to the North American future when the split between "artist" and "public" is complete and the artist will be totally ignored and let spin in a void of esoteric eliteness. Or on the other hand, judging from the way the "underground" (especially a type like Levy) remains ignored, it might be that in the future a neo-Higgins will splice on to psychedelia and reach out to the psychedelic-electronic "new masses" where the esoteric may be "generalized" and the dadaistic, futuristic forms in which Higgins is working will have become the forms of every day. There is something of "science-fiction" in the whole line of development from Tristan Tzara, the founder of Dada, all the way up to Higgins and Cage, something of Heisenbergian indeterminacy, moontrips and electronic chaos. It may be that Higgins is merely a presage of a brave new world that is yet to come—or, on the other hand, he may be merely one esoteric branch stuck out unnoticed in the void of High, High Culture in the Land of the Opulent, the Affluent, Glorified Masses.

Douglas Blazek ("Blaz"):
Steam-Engine Behind a Typewriter

Blazek is fast becoming the Grand Old Man of U.S. tough guy poetry. He represents a very violent reaction against the kind of poetry that was being produced in the U.S. before the Beat Revolution, poetry that was dead, academic, uninteresting, totally out of contact with the U.S. in the twentieth century.

I remember talking to Bukowski about Blazek one night. "He works in a factory," Bukowski said, "he's young, full of blood and fire. Life hasn't kicked the shit out of him yet." That was three years ago, and Blazek still not only survives, but begins to triumph.

Between 1964 and 1967 he edited a magazine called *Ole* and in 1967 after eight issues *Ole* stopped and Blazek published an *Ole Anthology,* Glendale, California: Poetry X/Change Press, 1967. In the introduction to this anthology he more or less outlines the whole of his aesthetics, a kind of Humphrey Bogart, back-alley, hard-knuckled neo-realism.

First of all, Blazek throws out the "academy:"

> We shun the word "literary;" it is the key to tea & donuts on Saturday afternoons. We have no need for parlor poetry that reinforces old ideas & comforting philosophies . . . . .

Blazek wants to take in all reality, nothing partial, slanted, filtered, "selected." He says essentially the same thing in an article that appeared in *Works* in the spring of 1969: "How could I continue ignoring beer cans in the park under my favorite willow tree?" From the beginning Blazek's aesthetics were militantly class-conscious, and stresses his own role as a proletarian poet:

> Great poets will no longer appear from an upper-middle class family that is financially comfortable. Poetry is no longer a luxury, it is a necessity! The struggling, fighting man is whose voice we will hear.

Poetry for Blazek is a revolutionary tool to be used against the repressive and carniverous society that surrounds us. Our society is a fraud and is turning us all into frauds, and poetry is a kind of sledgehammer to be used to break through the layers of fraud into the essential, the real. Echoing critics of the opulent society like Eric Fromm and Herbert Marcuse, Blazek sees poetry as a means of liberating ourselves from mind-control:

> It has brainwashed us so throughly that we are no longer warm human beings, but cold nonentities, neurotics, monomaniacs for artifacts & for the holy silver certificate . . . . We are sadists, confused, lost & willing to obey the ringing of the master's bell in D.C. or on Haight St . . . . But remember, there are still things to celebrate & the best celebration is expressed in song & the logical extension of song is a shout . . . . THEN SHOUT! Put your teeth into those words . . . . Sneak a peak between your crotch & see if you still have hair there. If there *is* hair, *say* there is hair. Don't hide the balls either. If there are balls then include the balls & make them look like balls, know they are balls. POETRY WITH BALLS! POETRY THAT IS

DANGEROUS! MEAT POETRY! Juice to make the
ears jump. . . . SOMETHING!

This was Blazek's great stand: Meat Poetry against the age
of the Enslaving Machine.

Charles Bukowski was the great precursor for this position.
Bukowski the post-revolutionary whose revolution was simply
to beat down the enslaving mechanisms of the world around
him by ignoring them, being totally his wild, profane, sensitive and giantsize self. Only the difference between Bukowski
and Blazek is that Blazek is *consciously* using his profanity
against the sacrosanct state, whereas Bukowski never really
gets around to a political stand, is merely and entirely himself.
Selfness seems to be enough for him, without any recourse
to a political stand or credo.

On the other hand, another Meat School Poet, Steve
Richmond, takes the whole Meat School position even
beyond Blazek's stand when he writes in his *Poetry Toward a
Creative Nonviolent Anarchy:*

> . . . . do you demonstrate?
> do you dig even the slightest political idea? do
> you even
> respect Che a little? Bonito Juarez? Hitler? Ghandi?
> Assholes
> like that? Oh
> they would shut me up
> for their purpose is control.
> limits on the mind, the mouth, the word
> as it has never been spoken.
> So what will I put on this paper . . . . Up your ass? Have you
> a plastic dick
> in your skull?   Can we exist without
> compromise?

Blazek and Richmond have a lot in common, although
Blazek is the more conservative of the two. Both of them,
starting from their own guts, their own bowels, vicera, intes-

tines, make a stand against mechanization, contrast modern plastic living with authentic, stripped down, essential experience. "Art has a tendency to detach itself from life," Blazek says in the introduction to the *Ole Anthology,* and his purpose is to get back to life, fight the media-world, the PR-centered, microwave world that slips right by flesh and blood:

> LIFE HAS ELUDED US—THE TV WAVES GOING
> THRU US ALL DAY LONG HAVE CONDITIONED
> US TO THINK LIKE HOLLYWOOD & ROCKEFELLER
> CENTER
> WE REASON & FEEL AS ADEPTLY AS THE LOWEST
> COMMON
> DENOMINATOR IN OUR SOCIETY. IT IS TIME FOR
> A CHANGE—
> OF DIET! WE NEED A NEW APPROACH TO INSIGHT
> THRU A
> NEW APPROACH TO POETRY.

Since the founding of *Ole* in 1964 Blazek really hasn't much changed from this basic stand in favor of LIFE and REALITY. He has, however, expanded and refined his position, especially in a book of letters published by Quixote called *Life in a Common Gun* (1968). Blazek writes a lot of poetry, but recently he has formed a kind of anti-poetry prejudice in favor of the letter as a new form of more honest, more basic communication. His new magazine, *Open Skull,* is just letters. As he explains in *Life in a Common Gun* (Madison, Wisconsin: Quixote Press, 1968), in a letter to Don Cauble:

> poetry is usually the distillment of a good letter, of a good thought, of a good experience. it is a dessicated skum bag left along the highway. we are all SO GOD-DAMN BLOODY ALIVE INSIDE but when it comes out in words on paper it stinks, it is a cripple, it is deformed, it is weak, *weak,* WEAK! the poem only seems to fancy-up the weakness, the cripple, by dressing it in the clothes of the poet, in the dreams & romanti-

> cism of spirituality—& let's not forget abtruceness. it's
> a religious puke! . . . the poet is a huckster who seems
> to only be able to stop playing games when he writes
> letters—& hardly even then. & this goes for everyone i
> know of whom i've read both their poetry & their letters.
> Buk's best writing is his letters. the letter aims out of the
> body—the poem aims inward. or///////so it seems!

Here Blazek begins to see the problem of "content" controlled by "form," but like many of the small, short revelations that Blaz starts out on, he lets this one also fall dead and
doesn't—as he might have—apply the same problem of real,
essential, viable communication to the other forms he so
much enjoys criticizing, namely the media. His stand against
poetry as formal exercise really is much the same as his stand
against films or TV or any other communication mode as
traditional form.

Blazek's problem though is that he never really sees himself
as an experimentalist, and in fact reacts violently to "experimentalism" as such as an unwanted form of High Culture.
This in turn keeps him confined permanently in the cage of
Low Culture which, in the age of curvilinear high-energy
packets, remains low energy and linear. When recently asked
about whether or not he was interested in moving into film,
TV, etc. he answered:

> . . . . . no i really don't see myself working into
> graphics or film or anything other than words. i know
> words are not the current rage, but i still have trust in
> them & sense that there are things that can be done with
> them which i have not yet done. i want to develop myself
> to the state of exhaustion & depletion. i guess the future
> starts *then!*

In his letters where he more or less lets go, however, the
proleteriat neo-realist often flows naturally and easily into a
kind of experimentalism that in trying to reach "reality,"

creates a highly complex word-construct style which I call "Graphic Associationism:"

> . . . . don't eat rice krispies on gray days. grayness is octopedal & strangulative—it is dope, uncut dope like milk is anti-dope. days like this are neither loveable or pitiable. they are long & slimmy. they are boils on the Pope's back. they are anthropological morticians, testing my flesh w/acid, sulphuric, nitric, hydrochloric—i am not under a slab under a cover glass or in a cauldron—i don't even have the covers of a white sheet on this bed yet alone over my body! . . . . . .

The associations here are rich and free-wheeling and highly graphic. Sequence is determined not by logic but graphic intensity. The primary rule followed is to pile associations on top of each other in an increasingly wide sensory spectrum that puts into gear the total sensory mechanism of the reader.

In a way Blazek is characterizing his own core-style in a description of Brown Miller's "poetnics" when he writes:

> you're doing things w/words that most everyone else is incapable of doing—in quantity & quality you use words in association to better communicate life's complexities than ordinarily is burdened upon our accepted method of using one word/symbol for each singular thing it symbolizes & then stringing together these singular symbols. you have realized that each thing in life that is symbolized is really a complexity of symbols ergo there must be an amalgam of words to come closer to the feeling & flavor of life—language becoming a concoction of unorthodox, experimented words spurning our taught logic but coming closer to the logic of life.

Here Blazek shows his debt to Beat theory and practice, especially that of Jack Kerouac who in his poetry (*Mexico City Blues*), and prose (*The Subterraneans, Doctor Sax*, etc.) follows a kind of lumping together of words practice very similar to that of both Blazek and Miller—although Blazek is much closer to Kerouac than Miller.

Word-form (structure), of course, is an expression of social-form (structure), and one really can't be re-formed (restructured) without the other. Blazek, like the Beats, feels that social re-formation should begin with semantic re-formation, and that once the semantic restructuring has begun then the rest of the social structure will slowly be reshaped and realigned. As he says in another letter to Brown Miller: "poetry . . . . must be able to bring about changes, otherwise it is a mere pasttime, a luxury, a hobby. Someday the time will come when being a poet will be very precarious, especially when writing hard hitting stuff *at* society *for* society out of love."

Blazek's own poetry suffers from the same symptoms that Blazek himself diagnosed as being inherent in poetry itself: an overawareness of form, an attempt to be poetic. This is especially true of his more recent work which has begun to move away from being a free-wheeling Tarzan-yell, into something almost as surrealistically polite as George Hitchcock:

> the Ten Gallon Cowboy
> rode into town like a gorilla
> & demanded his jungle back.
>
> the penguins dove underwater like fat bullets.
> the crocodilles played stuffed.
> the zebras were paintings.
> the giraffes hung with telephone wire.
> the coyote paced like a businessman.
> the monkeys gossiped by their tails.
> the hyenas gave their vulgar laugh.
>
> there is no more jungle, Cowboy . . . .
> ("Who's Who on Planet Earth")

The form-fracturing that he accomplishes so easily in his letters does not carry over into his poetry, and obsessed with a D. A. Wagner-like desire to simplify, clarify, reduce every-

thing to a tight, transparent form, in his poetry Blazek con-
fines himself to traditional Low Culture structures that have
more in common with the academic poetry that he is reacting
against, than the Pop Culture that he practices in his letters
(and life):

a day

a carton of smokes sits on
the bed next to the tarnished
mirror

the grayness of march
drains off the sky growing heavy
on the flesh—a gray joke—
i yawn & the city out the door
falls into a burlesque of itself

my brains were scattered over
yr body like worms of mud while
my soul sat in yr blouse like hot lead.
(part III, "The Commitment," *Sting and Die,* Eugene, Oregon: Toad Press, 1968)

Kerouac never sinned in the direction of Low Culture and
his poetry and prose hummed in an individualistic space
somewhere between Pop and High Culture. Being "revolutionary," his poetry was "difficult." But Blazek, caught up in
the cult of the New Clarity, traps himself in a highly rigid
structuralism that in turn disenables him to expand into the
thought-structures that he needs to have his poetry fulfill its
basically revolutionizing function. Without wanting to, he
slips into sentimentality:

I do not retreat

at this edge of being
I rest
like a zipper half zipped
waiting for the angels
that never seem to come

maybe they'll bring a roadmap?
("With My Skull as a Black Flag," from *I Advance With a
Loaded Rose* San Francisco: twowindows press, 1969)

or triteness:

everybody
was coming out of church.
you would think
that visiting a house
with the owner always absent
would discourage people—
they talk to the sky
the way they always
remembered it to be—
("Ramblings, of Sorts," from *I Advance With a Loaded
Rose*)

or metaphysical dadaism:

the phone scared me
into white woodwork
of electricity when
it rang once
("The Outrage of a Lonely Room," from *Sting & Die*)

At times, however, in spite of the confining set of rules that
he has set up for himself, Blazek does break through into a
solid expression of the "functionality" of a poetry that contains "warm flesh":*

there is something
about the walls
climbing over themselves
hands over teeth—
pipes & gutters

---

*In "My Definition of Poetry," Blazek writes: ". . . . I want/to be a bathtub/
. . . . always I would/contain warm flesh./always Iwould/be a function . . ."

zooming straight up.
I can't quite
get my hands around it.
it's the same feeling
I get walking into
washrooms of South Side
Chicago gas stations
cigarette butts & shoe
schuffings on
1932 lineoleum
derby hat grease feeling
& the sorrow
of gauze in Catholic hospitals:
holes where nails
used to sleep
the rusted torso
of an old cop car:
WHAT IS THIS?
WHAT AM I TRYING TO SAY?
it's not that
but what I *feel—*
I can feel
all the shoes
in a century of labourers
being laced
I can hear
more backs than bedsprings
creaking
("The Impossibility & the Wanting," from *I
Advance With a Loaded Rose)*

Here the proletariat, revolutionary poet, staying close
within the limits of simplicity, clarity, "essentialness," at the
same time somehow manages to "let go." The word-associa-
tion-piling that is *the* basic characteristic of Blazek's letter
style gets through: "derby hat grease feeling." The zany,
upsidedown subconscious logic of surrealism (". . . . the
walls/climbing over themselves/hands over teeth") is held in
just enough not to break the rhythm of cul de sac depression

that the poet is trying to convey. He is just elliptical enough ("I can hear/more backs than bedsprings/creaking") to break the headlong rush of reading-thinking . . . . and in an Eliotesque self-questioning ("WHAT IS THIS?? WHAT AM I TRYING TO SAY?") he steps out of the tough-guy role long enough to stand in front of the reader confused, uncertain, tentative and insecure.

In an article published in *Works* in the spring of 1969, Blazek lashes out with characteristic vigor at his old enemies, the academic poets "playing pin-the-tail-on-the-donkey, playing chess, strategy, knifing; each trying to out wit, out con, out do the other, each trying to create his own Morse code using handcrafted dots and dashes, designing elaborate code books, all done in style, *style,* STYLE, that would be consistent under the severest scrutinization."

Instead of this style-game, in much the same tone that he used in *Ole* back in 1964, Blazek offers poetry that is real, vital, alive:

> We need our poetry to be SOMETHING! If a cardboard box is beat up and sags then say it looks like your old Bulgarian grandmother with thick smelly stockings rolled up to her knees instead of comparing it to some Greek god that never existed in the first place. If you're going to write then write about things people can recognize, things that are REAL. If words don't have earth in them then they are as useless as a broken light switch.

Unfortunately Blazek identifies REAL with SIMPLE, when in fact his "realism" is basically an "un-" or "anti-" realism that tries to force the multi-channeled, omnidirectional, high-energy impacted reality of the world around him into not merely a traditional linear poetic expression, but one that is also ingenuously measured out in simple, clear word packages. Krech's simplicity is totally different because Krech never attempts to contain the complex world of his preceptions in any poetic form, merely throws out bits, fragments, sketches. Blazek, on the other hand, insists on a one to one ratio between simple form and the reality that that form is trying to convey, and in order to arrive at this ratio he is forced to reduce reality itself to one channel, one line, one wavelength. In spite of differences in content and form, then, between the "academics" and himself, Blazek by remaining lineal stays within the limits of Low Culture and retains much in common with the very academics he is fighting against. Like the academics he ignores huge areas of contemporary experience like economics, science, politics, technology, and stays outside of the experimental fringe areas of contemporary experience to concentrate on the essentially human in a context where the "human" has been intimately welded with the technological.

At the same time I suspect that Blazek, in spite of his unchanging manifestos in favor of the REAL, is in fact changing. When I first asked him for poetry for *The Living Underground: An Anthology,* he sent me a poem called "Schlitz" that begins like this:

> Schlitz—
> the tavern on Wells Street
> howling in oceans of night time,
> hard cunt messing with
> my flooded basement of blues
>
> the sluggish placenta
> liquid compost of blues. . . .

Which is strong, healthy stuff, but very much caged within the limitations the the Meat School mystique. You've got to get those four letter words in, they have to be there, you've got to be an American version of Brendan Behan, a real brawling bastard . . . very much like Bukowski, but with the difference that Bukowski doesn't take himself all that seriously.

But then recently, just before *The Living Underground* anthology came out, Blazek sent me another poem, "A Poem About Now," that reads:

This could be the last 3 minutes
we live—all we know and
understand abandoned like a flooded farm house,
evacuated like the Titanic.

Let us now take extraordinary measures
to save this world—after all,
3 minutes is a long time
for good men to motorize their
philosophy after many centuries
of conservative peddling (which
neither conserved men nor land) . . . .

There is a huge difference here. The barroom-Bukowski stance is replaced by an almost "literary" style (again the approaching the "academic"), and thematically instead of staying focused on the minutiae of "real" daily life, Blazek launches off into broad speculative themes about man and the cosmos.

I think that perhaps the whole Meat School approach was merely one step in Blazek's overall development. The Bogart-Bukowski stance was for the grandstands, but now after the grandstands have responded Blaz doesn't need them any more. He has appeared everywhere any contemporary poet wants to appear, *Chelsea, The Malahat Review, Arts in Society, The Smith, West Coast Review, Ann Arbor Review, San Francisco Earthquake, Vagabond, Trace, El Corno Emplumado, Illuminations, Wormwood Review* . . . . even *Kayak.* He has a whole string of books about to be published: *Survival Kit, Broken Knuckle Poems, Baptismal Corruption in the Sunflower Patch, Growth Is a Kangaroo Court.* Plus another batch waiting for a publisher. He himself is filled with an urgent sense of his own development. He doesn't want to be trapped, confined, limited. And as he writes in a recent letter (10/29/69):

. . . . i feel there is a rather narrow image of me at the present which would be greatly enlarged if the next five years could be fitted into the next 5 minutes.

Certainly Blazek's direction *seems to be* toward an increased scope, theme- and diction-wise. He is painfully aware of experimentation and High Culture as his "Homage to the Square, the Blacks, Ian Hamilton Finlay & Marshall McLuhan" (you open up a card and there's this black square—nothing else) shows. One of the answers might be a little well-controlled complexity—"rich ambiguity. The letters really show the multi-levelled photon-gun quickness of Blazek's mind, where the essential Blazek really is. The next step might very well be to extend this multi-levelled approach out into his theory, and eventually into his poetry itself. At this point in his development he can really afford to go anyway he wants, and his only sure death as a poet-critic would be to simply stand still.

D. R. Wagner: The Great "Poser"

On one level D. R. Wagner is a simple flower child who writes something like Krech—only without Krech's fanatical clarity—about love and nature and the basic goodness in man:

> your sleeping is
> as children in
> the afternoons
> of all my peace
> and the words
> rest softly in
> your mouth.
>
> All that is beautiful
> sleeps around you
> and I can not touch
> you with my closed
> down mirrors.
> (*Book for Barb*, 1967)

His mind flies high, mundane reality flips out into kiddy-kar gymnastics and the surrealistic fire alarm begins to ring all over the page:

> Here were lovers caught in each others hair
> and singing with voices like stoves and eyes

that darted like a violence of dying clothes
hanging in the wind . . .

On the land a freeway was truly free and threw
cars off its back and bolted for the hills
trailing whistles and police cars in its train.
And the trains. ran without rails, their wheels
chewing holes into the fields people with blue
ducks. The heart of the land rang free.

There was no reason to leave anywhere for anywhere.
He boarded the plane and Los Angeles was a magic city.
The robes flew away and he never saw the way they went.
(*Amper&and,* March, 1969)

Wagner's flower-child love poems are elfin and coy, suffused with guaranteed, bonafied, 100% transcendental-buddhistic ingenuousness. They are filled with mystical overtones of almost lost Catholicism which Wagner has converted into pure "Luv-ism" without a touch of the taint or hurt of original sin. For example, the prefatory note in *The Footsteps of the Returning King That Have Been Lost to Us for Such a Long Time It Seems Like They Never Were and Other Poems* (1968): "Some of these poems have previously appeared at Lourdes and Fatima."

In *The Footsteps,* Wagner's girl, Barb, is transformed into a transcendent Virgin-Beatrice symbol who leads Wagner (Dante) through his initiation into the Vita Nuova . . . the New—purified, love-centered—Life:

> Barbara . . . . .
> Why is it yr name
>   makes it so easy
>   for angels to go to sleep?

Barb cancels out Wagner's ego ("I am feeling/your breath/across my I's") and brings him back to the Edenic world before the Fall, the Golden Age when passion was good and order was a "natural" component of man's inner nature:

> I have these wonderful thing [sic]
> to give to you if you will
> promise
> to sing me a song about
> how everything was before
> this world stuck its fat ass
> in the window and shit
> all over the table.

At the same time, though, even this transfigured world of simple innocence and pure light is touched with smudges of the other, fallen world (the Freudian phylogenetic subconsciousness) and Wagner evades any psychic-penetration encounter that might reveal the other, "fallen" side of his nature:

> If I speak to you of my dreams
> will you not go into them to find
> broken dolls and the little leadweight
> things that make their eyes close when
> ever they are sleeping.

All he wants to be reminded of is the "graces" bestowed by love performed in an unsullied flowerworld:

> Should I forget,
>   remind me of what
> kind of flowers
> made yr back
>   smell so good
>   after we loved
> in those fields.

As you begin to move down through the various layers of Wagner's mind, he becomes not only increasingly complex, but also increasingly aware of evil. Wagner is a kind of "inverted" Dante, and instead of moving up and out of the *inferno* to a *paradiso* of mystical rose beatitude, as we move through his work we descend to lower and lower obsessive hell-levels of existential obsessiveness until in the final, lowest level we come up against a wall of total incommunicability designed to prevent the passage of any and all meaning.

In *The Sirens in the Park and the Ribbons in the Hairs* (1968), subtitled "Four from the Flesh," all flower-thoughts, all innocence and "purity" are left behind and we enter the level of "sex-torture" where the celebration of sexual pleasure is inverted and twisted into prolonged agony.

There are four episodes, the first about a girl getting "felt up" in a movie. She doesn't reach a climax from being felt up, though, but alone, just before the film ends, while watching the film itself—a scene of soldiers massacering Indians. The violence, the morbidity of the massacre create a substitute-orgasm stronger than the real thing:

> the bullets ripping through
> their coats and his hand
> inside moving and the joy of
> the bullets and hot

The second episode is about a girl getting it for the first time, and here Wagner makes a definite step towards semantic anti-communication mumbo-jumbo. We are in the girl's mind. She's not so much hurt as "numbed," she slips out of sequential grammar, her mind clots up, twists, spasms:

> and she nod
> him gently and
> did the things
> the books had said
> was done
>   all the while
>   being hungry
>   and why him

The split begins between the fragmented, disjointed agonizing "person," and his whole communication structure. The "hunger" and the awareness of repeating "book-actions" represent social, "outside" structures unrelated to the inner existential structure of essential, personal need.

The third episode, just a little bit further along in a graduated scale in increasing violence, allows the violence itself to remain hanging in a word-web on intentional vagueness. The theme is essentially the same—sexual violation—but here we are not told exactly what happened, merely that the man took "too much" from the woman and was "unable to put it back," and that she "could not/move at all." Here the sex-act paralyzes, destroys . . . . and the individual is hopeless against its maleficent power. The woman tries to move, tries "to reach/out," and the man—in an act of senseless automatism—leaves "the room to run water/in the sink."

The last of these "flesh episodes" is the most mute, condensed, disjointed:

"sad?"

and nothing else

some breathing

only because she

could not stop it

and lifted herself

up covering

"no?" the word.

"what then?"

but it was already too
late and he lit two cigarettes
and she told him he was
thoughtful
and he figured he was pretty
good and she knew he wasn't
but could not tell him
him being warm and her
guts hurting so.

Communication is "interiorized," reduced to the barest elements of self-contained hurt. The lowest level in this non-communicative circle in Wagner's *inferno* is that of silent suffering. The male-female split is complete, the man invincibly ignorant in his sense of "maleness," and the girl retreating, withdrawing into fragile, delicate and sullen "femaleness." *The Footsteps of the Returning King* . . . . is an ode to bi-sexual communication, an interpersonal openness that inevitably leads to a sense of "cosmic" participation. The individuals in tune with themselves, are *able* to affix themselves to the larger life of the world around them. *The Sirens in the Park* . . . . . represents the other side of this communication coin. Interpersonal communication comes to a complete standstill. Sex, instead of being a "road," becomes a "wall." Individuals are totally trapped in "roles," and persons submerged in "the things/the books had said was done."

In the *Putah Creek Overflow,* Wagner confronts the problem of incommunication on an even more essential level—that of language structure itself. The prefatory note—"prepared in an edition of 200 copies for friends of the *English Language*"—is indicative of the demolition tactics that Wagner uses to destroy the sematic envelope of the basic "attitudes" and "structures" that he is attacking. The *Putah Creek Overflow* is a declaration of deep cynicism and despair in which the love-flower communication flow is replaced by a jammed, clotted, twisted incommunication just one step away from a total abandonment of language as communication.

It begins with a scene similar to that in *The Sirens*. . . . only more abstract, merely a scene of "bars" between a man and a woman. The girl asks the man his name and pushes "several/dead leaves/between them." He holds up a sign "I AM BLIND." She sex-teases him ("She sirred/him generous/and exposed her dove") and he holds himself up against the bars, whistles and thinks "snakes/and other/blind thoughts."

Here Wagner has entered into a kind of shorthand cubism.

There are no really "total" objects, but merely angled "surfaces," line-people who aren't really people at all but pure
symbols, the seducer pitted against the seductress, neither of
them "communicating" but merely exposing their stereo-
typed, "other-created" symbolic selves.
In the next poem (all part of an untitled, unnumbered "sequence") Wagner moves from cubism into semantic dis-
tortion and forces the reader to fasten, not on the "sense,"
but the "form" (or "anti-form") itself:

"OH you must"

end he said finally
I thought it was ewe
that smelled
this farm and all
around us being

she sithered his
innane remarks on
the walls of the building
and repeated the land
which he promptly burned
mumbling to himself
the must be easier ways
to make a loafing than
baking my back

peach day.

The purpose of "peach day" instead of "each day," "to
make a loafing" instead of "making a living," etc. is to schizophrenically destroy "meaning" by ignoring words as inter-
related communication symbols. They become chance sound-
interrelationships ("ewe"-"you," "peach"-"each") confined
to their own structure on the page. The page-world becomes
detached to its own ends and purposes, and Wagner's art
stops talking about other people, other worlds, other contents
and contexts. Wagner, abandoning his role as Dantesque pilgrim, begins to become an anti-god, creating anti-worlds of

self-enclosed anti-meaning. He is on the edge of Dada, close to Higgins' aleatic world of pure form.

In the "Yolo Causeway,"—"(a given to Brown Miller)"—normal word-sense is completely displaced by this world-in-itself word game. Thematically the "Yolo Causeway" is close to the usual Wagnerian obsessiveness with an unsatisfied, forced, painful sex act.

The girl refuses to have sex with the boy ("she/poppingly worded him/to leave her alone"), he leaves ("trick, trick he/pricked and left right/away"), then returns, she asks him to make love to her . . . and then dies. The boy stands thinking for a moment and then leaves:

he thought
for a long
moment
twice and
turned
to leave.
leaving.
left.

This sameness in thematic structure, however, conceals vast differences in technique. Added to the puns and sound-plays ("tried/to smell something of/the heir in the room," "butt all had gone up/in smoke") is a tightly knit semi-surrealism filled with symbolic innuendos that are purposefully interpretation-resistant:

from the perhaps on her tongue
he brushed a large bug
from his hat and waited
for the train to come.
engine sneaks into
the station coughs twice
and leaves them repeating
each other until dark.
the streetlights also leaving.

Separate objects merge—the perhaps on her tongue, the large bug on his hat—and lose their separate identities in a gesture of mutual cancellation. People and objects are pulled toward each other and interpenetrate. The puffing engine transfers its "puffingness" to the station ("the station coughs twice") and the station in turn transfers this same echoing, repetitive "puffingness" to the couple ("leaves them repeating/each other . . . ."), and then as their litany-like reenforcement of their own identities shuts off at dark, the streetlights, the light-bearers, also leave, and the whole micro-cosmos involved in the poem rushes into a solid, tightly packed state of total anihilation. The girl dies and the boy leaves (". . . . leave./leaving/left./) the world to death and darkness.

This is the final stage of Wagner's incommunication: the destruction of all object-knower relationships, the narrowing of the epistomological gap between "knower" and "known" until the two "blend" and with the blending all consciousness is cancelled out by the "things" themselves.

Recently Wagner has been flirting rather seriously with concrete poetry—the treatment of words, not as communica-tion-units, but as plastic (decorative) design-elements. This graphics development is really the logical direction of Wag-ner's whole artistic career. No matter how he managed to manipulate words, no matter how much he fought against meaning, he never escaped from his obsessiveness with "dirty sex."

The "broken dolls" hidden in his dreams in *The Footsteps* represent an obsessive leitmotif that carries through all of Wagner's work. His increasingly cloudy and warped word-manipulation, on the other hand, is his attempt not so much to exorcise but cover over this monomania.

Never able to really communicate a "message," Wagner remained trapped within the cage of his own sense of shame and guilt, and as he began to see the same "formula" appear and reappear over and over again he tried to erase the for-mula with increased crypticness . . . . but never to the point that he allowed himself to cover up the "formula" entirely. The "formula" had to be stated, because only through a public statement could he hope for the "catharsis" (expiation) that was the basic motive for publishing these poems in the first place.

Unlike the rest of the Underground, Wagner never was able to extend himself out far enough to identify with a really "social" consciousness. Under the love-child surface was a shamechild enclosed within shame to such an extent that a sense of "group," of "political" or "movement" awareness never really had a chance to develop.

Recently Wagner has been moving more and more into visual (graphic, concrete) poetry. He is curator of the Sacramento State College art museum, and has been developing a whole new "craft" as a visual poet. At the same time this kind of total visualization is very much within Wagner's whole line of artistic development. By moving into total visualization, Wagner has at last been able to escape from the twisted obsessiveness of his sick "love"-content, and replace content with a complete concentration on form. The message is no longer important, but the way "it's done." The "it" has been replaced by the "how." Words disappear and "things" take over.

And now that "content" as such has been eliminated, it may be that the "curse" will be lifted from Wagner's head, and he will be able to slowly replace his fixed obsessiveness with whole new slants of "implied content." In visual poetry in a sense the "message" in itself is blocked by "form." Even if he wants his guilt to come through, the media itself goes against any such exposure, and freed from the possibility of communication, Wagner may be released from his own past and begin to "non-communicate" in completely new directions. Wagner will probably offer more suprises, more radically new development in the next few years than any other poet in the Underground.

Similar to Brown Miller in his use of poetry as a medium of exorcism, Wagner has always seen the "poem-reality" as a concentrated, slow-motion kind of "slide-viewer." In a recent issue of *Panama Gold* (July, 1969) there appears a poem of Wagner's called "It's Kind of What Death is Like," all about a tree (penis) moving toward a girl outside of the "door of the house where she lived" (vagina):

> . . . . . the girl moved backward, the pond spilled toward
> her,
> the sun swirled and mixed in leaves and feathers.

At this point in the "reality-orgasm," Wagner retreats and writes a poem about what he has seen:

> . . . . . I slid into a chair, stuck a piece
> of paper in my machine and slowed the whole thing down
> just to see how it looked.

In other words, "free reality" escapes Wagner and he needs to process and control it in order to understand it. At the same time contentwise his universe even symbolically revolves around a very limited pre-determined set of phallic elements.

The question now is if Wagner by switching "media" will be able to vary content . . . . or will his visual poetry merely represent visual variations of content too deeply rooted inside him to ever be really escaped. At any rate, Wagner's "machine"—whatever machine he uses—should provide many interesting watching hours in the years to come . . . . . he obviously is an artist who is unable to stand still, fix himself in any one stance and hold it for any time at all.

Don Cauble: Reality-Fanatic

In Cauble's 1968 volume *Inside Out* (Portland: Dead Angel Press), there is a poem called "A Dream, Perhaps?" which provides the key to his entire aesthetics. The poem is all about an obsession he has with a particular blonde. He wants to get rid of her, get her out of his mind. . . . but he can't. And not only that but her reality (memory, mind reality) is as real as the reality immediately surrounding him (proximate, sensory reality):

> I taste blonde hair.
> real as the black marks
> on this page
> as the macroni i ate
> just minutes ago.
> real as the book
> i walked downtown
> to buy this morning.

Mind-reality here is primarily gustatory, then tactile ("my poems/lush/the sweat from yr skin"), then kinesthetic ("my body—/lovecome hammered into/words") . . . and he feels himself trapped in this intimate, immediate, closely encircled sensory world.

He wants to abstract this reality, shift it into a more generalized symbol-system, but is unable to:

> . . . . . if I could dissolve you
> into the Sea—
> an escape,
> a drowning!
> but you refuse to dissolve,
> to melt.

He tries to tranform the blonde into "light" ("even now/ I'm transforming/you/into Light,/dissolving yr hair/& bones/into pure color"), but that doesn't work either. Reality as such resists any kind of abstraction-manipulation, and he finally comes to regard the very process of abstraction itself as a process of falsification whereby the "real" is transformed into an "unreal" symbol world of "ghosts" and "spirits."

Instead of moving from "objects" to "symbols," Cauble sometimes moves backwards from "symbols" (symbolic objects) to specific "objects" themselves. His movement is always back towards "thing-in-itselfness," away from abstracted "mind-interpretation-of-thingness." In "Drowning I Think Must be a Long Way to Walk," he crosses a street, a light flashes and a woman is suddenly evoked:

> . . . . the light flashes
> I cross
> & yr mouth
> circles
> me
> into the blond curve
> of yr throat
> yr legs open to my
> fingers
> yr eyes
> close.

A letter in his hands metamosphoses into a woman "in bed

naked/with yr husband/& dreaming." Nothing ever really transcends Cauble's own ego-boundaries, but everything curves and folds back in on itself, enclosing and limiting him in an unbreakable mind-world of his own fashioning.

As far as intentions are concerned, Cauble "intends" to—as he says in a recent letter to me—"pull everything together into the image which will UNFOLD & EXPAND w/in YOU MIND so that you can EXPERIENCE IT."

The multiple unfolding, untwisting concrete images are part of a planned invasion of the reader's consciousness. Cauble is actually re-creating on the page—and in the reader's mind—the immediacy of reality as he perceives it in all its uncensored, unfiltered impact.

This explains much of the "over-done," "over-loaded," "over-impacted" imagery in his work, passages like:

> hardons tear cobwebbed panes
> of a movie house,
> lift in secret
> her slick smooth flesh
> & staple her rag-clot heart
> into cigarette smoke dreams . . . .
> (from "Six by Three Fold-Out Visions of Death")

Here Cauble is trying to "generalize" his one-shot concrete imagination into a kind of summed-up, coupled-together statement of specific facts.

The poem is about a sexual experience he is having with a girl who reminds him of Marilyn Monroe. His specific experience stays specific and combines with a generalized sex-death symbolic statement whereby the specific is interpenetrated with the "general" and, as elsewhere, the "general" (abstract) is violently pulled down and fastened onto the specific. Without ever losing the impact of the specific (concrete) Cauble converts a highly individual sexual experience into a general cultural-sexual statement: "I crash through broken eye glasses/the Golden Disc fear & desire,/her Marilyn Monroe face melts,/dripping candles into my hands./silk thighs like mad dogs/split heart & head."

Cauble's most impressive use of this "specific-generalization," though, occurs in poems like "Even God Must be Lonely at Night" or "Love Outside the Asylum" (both in *Inside Out*) where he projects himself into *someone else's private world-vision,* and is able to evolve—much in the manner of Browning's dramatic monologues—the development and extension of multiple concrete world-views.

Cauble very seldom selects any "normal" world-view as a subject for presentation. "Even God . . . ." for example, is about a girl obsessed by spiders ("the blonde girl could hear the/legs of the fuzzy spiders crawling over the/walls.") whose hands, as she masturbates herself, gradually combine both hand- and spider-identity:

> the girl slipped her small hands down
> below her belly . . . she closed her eyes & touched small
> hands to her wiry blond nest. now the spiders
> had crossed the room. without seeing them
> she knew they had reached the bed. she could
> hear their soft wet prayers, she could feel
> their furry legs slowly crawling & crawling.
> crawling up her legs. crawling

Of course this identity-merging is, in one sense, merely another variation of Cauble's whole drive toward imminence and immediacy . . . . . "objectification." "Things" are combined to emphasize and augment the psychological impact behind the actual concrete happening. The girl, alone in the desperation of her own solitude, mixes her phobias with her hidden, guilty desires so that the desires themselves are little more than guilty, phobic reactions, and Cauble in order to concretize the impact of this phobic-desire synthesis, actually turns the girl's hands into spiders.

In "Love Outside the Asylum," the presentation technique is much simpler, similar to the "interview" techniques used by, say, Jean Luc-Goddard or Andy Warhol when they merely move a sound-camera into a scene and start "recording reality." This is merely reality as it happens, ingenous, non- (not anti-) logical, a bit flat, even bland:

> when I was seventeen,
> she said,
> I went to Boston
> alone in a dirty green room.
> I fell in love with a homosexual
> he lived across the hall
> we walked along the Charles
> in autumn rain
> crystalling orange burnt leaves
> against iron fences
> La Jete will I ever forget that damn movie?

As always, Cauble avoids "square" subjects. He likes people who flirt with death ("I wanted to take the whole bottle/but didnt/they would not kill me"), who want to escape, retreat into themselves ("I stumble in/to climb & fall again/all the structures I've built/to hide in, destroyed/poems/air mail letters/pictures taped to the walls/myself"), people trapped in inescapable traps ("backing up/until theres no backin/space"). As in the work of Kryss or Levy or even Brown Miller, the world that emerges is filled with fixations, desperate retreats, large fears.

The underground poets as a whole present a psychogram of the U.S. that is depressed, downtrodden, frightened, "trapped." In a sense they are the "advance-conscience" of the rest of the summed-up psychomass of U.S. culture, expressing today what the less sensitive areas of this psychomass (over-psyche) will feel in the near future. Cauble as a psychotype of the U.S., feels "threatened," a surrealistically stewed-together kind of threatening that expresses itself in the fear of "Local Gang Leaders" (violence), of having his name splashed across theater marquees (bogus-value publicity), of

never reaching any definitive or final goal (frustration of
value-achievement in a goalless society). . . . .
Although *Inside Out* does have some strong social (mass,
group) implications, however, its strength lies in its very nar-
rowness. The mass-outcry can be derived from the individual,
but for the most part the individual remains precisely that:
solitary, unitary, alone. In *Early Morning Death Fragments*
(1969), on the other hand, Cauble loses a great deal of "force"
by leaving the subjective, individual howl behind and becoming an objective "social critic." He no longer depends on the
prototypicality of his own gut-reactions, but "objectifies,"
puts the problems on the table and studies them at a distance:

> Head hunters are dragging blondes
> & ripping them to pieces:
> Miss America throws away the keys:
> I'm scrambling on the floor
> with the lights out
> but she only laffs & says
> You won't find anything there!
> she takes me inside
> & shows me thru the prison.
> the sparrows are being fatted
> & she says Wont you please stay?
> ("The Center")

Here Janet, the "fallen angel" of Inside Out, is replaced by
Miss America and he, Don Cauble, the persecuted paranoid
poet, is replaced by "the sparrows" that are being fattened for
the slaughter. The message is no longer bone-marrow and
nerves, but a contrived, generalized "symbol system" that
really contradicts Cauble's own individualistic poetics.

Still, in spite of his overt symbolizing in *Early Morning
Death Fragments,* Cauble's message retains a great deal of
force. This message, found in the title poem, is simply that the
U.S. is a hollow, separate-people society that has lost its ability to love. Cauble's partial-answer is the rediscovery of
"flesh," "love," "the unity of two-people-made-one":

our own bodies I've discovered
are not so ugly naked
when naked with someone else.
& while we're naked,
lets make luv.

the only cure is human cure
& one person does not make a human.

This "breaking of separateness," though, is only one part of Cauble's answer. In *Inside Out,* in a poem called "Somewhere Between Streets and Asylum Wax-Stocked Girlflesh Torments and Wet Eye Focuses," Cauble stresses the need for discovering "the God/within us." We try to kill him, but he can't be killed, and slowly, in spite of ourselves, this "godself" unfolds inside us:

we push water & land thru
sun into plant,
into fish,
cats stretch in the sun.
women roll over in dreams
& the moon makes luv to a cloud.
we whisper
& we're alone
with ying & yang fingers
they're slowly closing their fists
& when we come into them
theres no flash only ourselves.

In his more recent poetry Cauble has moved further and further "inside," looking for—and finding—this other, this "divine," this "alternate" self:

In & out are dreams
of the past,
he says,
you see . . . for us . . . .
theres only ourselves
("Standing Still," manuscript poem)

Some of the stock characters of *Early Morning Death Fragments*—Tom and Becky, Miss America—still appear, and some new characters—Saj, the Grave Keeper, Blue Giant, One Eyed Jane—are added, but now the drama has all been internalized by mind-expanding drugs, and all conflict and development take place within a floating dreamworld context of pure vision and hallucination. "Things" still predominate (Cauble as he moves further inside himself does not abandon his customary "concreteness") but now they are filled with intense hallucenogenic radiation:

> Saj builds a fire
> then turns the house inside out.
> he gives free passes
> to all the angels.
> he writes on the walls
> YOU CAN GO AS FAR IN
> AS YOU CAN GO OUT.

The outlines of Cauble's new acid-world are fairly clear, the psychodrama being reacted is rather obvious. In a sense the acid mindworld is a kind of highly souped up and inverted (insideouted) looking-glass version of the same factors that were operative before Cauble went acid.

The mind-garden is "surrounded by dogs./a cop shouts./well whatcha waitin' for???" Acid or no acid the menacing police-station remains the same. Also, the need for "love" doesn't essentially change, although the whole tone of the love-need is more relaxed, lower-tensioned, lower-pressured:

> I worry about coming
> when I've already left!
> Its all the same!
> laffs One Eyed Jane.

Sex is not merely genital, but a wider sensory (skin) experience that enables the experiencer to move into higher states of "being":

> All suns have strings,
> cries Vanessa.
> I grab her
> & the lights go out.
> Not that way! she says.
> Here . . . . . & punches holes
> thru her skin . . . . . Look!

Here sex is merely a "string" (means) for pulling down the "sun" (mystical "high"), and as Vanessa, the mystical adept, says to Cauble, the neophyte, not the usual way . . . . you move through the skin into "sun experiences," mystical states.

Cauble, in a sense, is on the threshold of a whole new inner-world development. He is a novice who sees the inner pool of placidity deep inside his mind, but who still is not able to reach it. He is a mystic becoming aware of his own mysticism, a guru beginning the long journey toward total guruhood. Only he can't break out of the "first circle" of attachement to the particular, the concrete, the individual. Even interiorized inside him "things" still persist in impeding his progress down to the calmer, sense-freed level of being:

> Its all in yr head anyway!
> Yeah, I know . . . . moans the Prisoner,
> thats why we're still here!
> ("Deadwood with Screaming Roots," manuscript)

Only the promise of deeper inner penetration remains. Cauble feels he will make it "in," conducted "in" by Becky (Tom Sawyer's Becky) who becomes a kind of Beatrice (again echoes of Wagner) ready to bring him down through the circles inside him to the total-calm center of his "self":

Tom runs screaming down the halls.
LET ME IN! LET ME IN!
In time . . . . Becky whispers . . . . . in time!

By extension this movement to the inner mystical being-poll inside of Cauble is symbolic of a larger movement of American "dissatisfaction" and "frustration" into a new historical period of renewed "innocence." Cauble's constant manipulation of the Becky-Tom symbols is an attempt on his part to reenact in terms of cultural history, the whole mystical play that is taking place within himself. Cauble as a duplicate ego of Tom Sawyer sees himself as a symbol of America's whole lost innocence attempting to re-find itself. The present is repressive ("pigs set up house in the garden"), the poet visionaries like Levy destroy themselves by seeing reality too clearly ("paranoid street cleaners/murder Cleveland's first prophet/w/his own 22 vision") . . . . . the point is that the reality itself must be changed. Cauble cannot retreat into himself the way he wants and is prevented from retreating by the hard fact of the nature of this "outer" repressive reality. So that the inner (mystic) and the outer (cultural-historical) are dependent on each other and for Cauble to reach acid-heaven, his cultural-historical double, Tom Sawyer, must be reinstated in the socio-economic heaven of overall U.S. cultural reform.

Cauble's latest poetry is certainly his most interesting. His earlier work is very much trapped in literalness, even if that literalness is the literalness of madness. Now his work "floats" and "gambols" in the free air of omni-possible acid-circuits. Image- and association-wise, his work has been liberated from consecutive reality:

Jane tells you
shes from the other side
& cant get back
thru all the traffic
lace curtains are blown

over yr face
you stare at the ceiling
& run yr hands up the walls.
("With One Foot in the Grave the Fool Pauses & Dreams
He's Dancing," manuscript)

In a sense Cauble is where Levy was when he committed suicide, stigmatized by the fact of being a visionary, at the same time possessed by the kind of horrendous, screaming vision that he realizes cannot change until the whole visionary-source-field around him changes too. Cauble is very dependent on his immediate milieu. If he weren't, if he could detach himself from the socio-economic context of the world around him, his visions could become totally personal, introverted, self-involved. He could become a mystic oblivious to the world around him, his only fight the fight to break into the energy-charged "cloud of unknowing" that is the ultimate revelation.

But the American mystic is first American, then mystic, and unable to fold in on himself and exclude his awareness of the "common-wealth" *or* common-poverty. The American poet-mystic is tied unconditionally to his sense of community, group, "society," and unable to free-float in the selfness of his own insulated ego. He cannot exclude "the other" from the radius of his own imaginings, but is forced to imagine, to dream, even to "trip out," tied to the multicellular, guilty sense of "otherness."

As thermometer-barometer, poet Cauble tells us a great deal about the interior climate of the republic:

the mad historian crashes
a burning time machine
thru back alleys
that curve into each other
like acid freeways
flashing Van Gogh EXITS

The time-machine is burning and the historians (especially

the "media-historians") have gone mad. The great tragedy, however, is that Cauble—like Levy—sees the only way out down "acid freeways/flashing Van Gogh EXITS," because all Van Gogh exits lead flat smack up against the dead-ends of mute suicide.

John Oliver Simon: Myth-Maker

In a sense John Oliver Simon is the "prototype" of the whole hippy movement . . . . or not just the hippy movement, but the entire movement of what might be termed American "pro-spiritualism" that had its roots in nineteenth century transcendentalism, and was submerged in the pessimism of naturalism until it was rediscovered by the Beats in the 1940's. Although still in his early twenties, Simon is a kind of Old Man of the Mountain, the Zen-Thoreau-Snyder Master whose early poetry at least came out unintentionally charged and fused with "sacred," scriptural overtones:

I'd like you to see

blacknight, birds
talking
with animal skins

arranging the stars.

green flowers
orange flowers
cactus red wax flowers
all in the morning.

this is in my darkest house.
("San Francisco Street Poems," No. 8, *Roads to Dawn Lake,* Berkeley: Oyez, 1968, p. 64)

Simon's work all centers around the "myth" of the return through multiple layers of languaged civilization to the core of primal mute animal-sound "nature." For Simon the quest for self-realization necessitates passing through "civilization" to an identification with man's inner primate-animal level, out into the other side of "primateness"—the wordless unity of man and world on the level of raw being.

Simon's starting point is already back out away from the "present." His quest begins with a departure from civilization, back to the essential (primitive). "The stone narrows to a dark door" and he moves through the stone-door, not to co-existence, but co-essence, even coalesence, with the savage. The North American Indians, for example, in retreating from the white man, interpenetrated more and more with nature, and the deeper the interpenetration, the greater their self realization:

> the Indians took to the mountains.
> they learned to live in the snow.
> in the canyon, left their sentinels:
> hammered on a dark rock, the sun's face,
> the white eye and dancing hair.
> ("Superstition Canyon," *Roads,* p. 3)

Nature for him moves at a different time than civilized time. It is slower, more elementally meaningful . . . . and it is the pace, the change-rate, that he himself aspires to:

> after walking fifteen miles
> I thought as slow as rock,
> taking the air, rain, light
> in a dim language.
> ("Travelling," *Roads,* p. 6)

While travelling through this "mythic," "dream" time, Simon puts behind him his learned language and like a new Adam tossed out alone on a primordial world that needs naming, he arrives at the name-roots of things, their special inspace, *haeccittas,* thisness:

> now I
>> can make the
>> first names of a
>> few things. give me
>>> your hands. and
>>> I will tell you.
>
> ("Mt. Clark Poem," *Roads,* pp. 16–17)

He moves back through time, leaves the U.S. with its Indian past and moves down through layers of other civilizations to find a basic "human" cultural unity, the cultural silence that pre-dates word-language:

> the silences outside of the poem
> are more important
> as if I touched your
> thigh, gently
> while I said this
>
> King Minos dances with his
> war-tools
> the Athenians lay their black clothing carefully in my mind.
> ("Lykabettos, Athinai" *Roads,* p. 42)

He anticipates sign-language, the return back to "now" and "America," bringing with him the knowledges of other time-zones and other intuitions:

> what to speak with my
> hands when I come
> back, they have known other
> woods, earths, water
>
> written in the rain, Kibbutz Magal
> (No. 6 of the "Magal Poems" *Roads,* p. 54)

By losing himself in diversity ("I am bearded/inside. walk

to other/rhythms in an unknown shape") he arrives at an all-inclusive, summing-up, creative "unity." He arrives at the primordia of things, the beginnings of forms, shapes half uttered, caught mid-way in the creative processes of definition:

> lie down underneath
> listen to new
> moon. listen to sun edge
> down and black fishing boats
> spiral
> green tides, white dark babies dream under fathoms
>
> under keel, dark
> carved animal bodies
> elkhorn
> deerfeet, horses many houses
> black pine, fishing boats
> (Untitled, *Roads,* p. 56)

All through his mythic journey (". . . . the myth requires/the journey"), though, Simon is obsessed by a sense of futility. He is not Christ (time-transcending), but Man-Satan (time-trapped), turned in on himself, formed in his own image, overwhelmed by time, and never able to really break out of his self-shell:

> now on the horned
> mountain, I am poor
> Satanas named for the morning
> each time, the innocent, changed
> in my own likeness.
> ("The NEW HEAVEN to those who stand on the NEW
> EARTH," *Roads,* p. 13)

To really be one with nature would be to fully accept change ("change: all beasts are happy,/caught in a trap of/bones, sing in snake's mouth/not corrupted") and all that this acceptance implies: an unawareness of self apart from natural being-in-time change. The New Earth that Simon seeks is precisely his own "unconsciousnessing," his immersion in "selfness," "unselfconscious" time, like the deers he saw "dancing/a pattern, in the morning between peculiar stones." The "language of the body" that he speaks of is the wordless language of time-acceptance whereby the individual subordinates his self ("Satanas named for the morning") to the innocence of organic cosmic unity:

> where you have brought me
> Worlds, in the
> mists below my feet:
> Give me the Kingdom
> in the first
> language of the body.
> ("The NEW HEAVEN," *Roads*, p. 14)

At most this kind of unity can be partial and intermittent, interrupted by the intrusion of the "other"—civilized—world.

Dancing Bear (1969) represents a big change in Simon's attitude. *Roads to Dawn Lake* had ended with the promise of an increased, heightened growth of perception. The journey of at-one-ment (at-one-ness) had begun. The mystic-poet had surrendered himself to the "nature forces," undergone his purification, and had moved into the new place of "enlightenment:"

> in the black moon I was dead
> I drank for three days
> on the mountain
> waters. on my head these
> pretty flowers for the other kings.
>
> I have taught you.
> the four kings and rivers
> are moving while I sleep.
>
> it has begun.
> ("at the rock-crack, stair/in the rock . . .," *Roads*, p. 72.)

Although the "presence" of the world always made itself felt through the quest in *Roads* ("My killdeer was plywood and metal/and the country was bounded by owners"), somehow Simon had managed to outdistance civilization, leave Kryss' technological-slum-world behind, and manage to breathe pure mountaintop (purifying) air. In *Dancing Bear,* on the other hand, the here-and-now world breaks the mystic communion with strong political noise. We are in Krech's latest world, the politics of survival, not salvation:

> chasing cop tripped & the human
> mask flew open, blonde sun
> glasses revealed the sex crime
> helmet & club shot loose
> across the pavement
>
> to where I was waiting
> like an old fox on thin ice pond
> in northern mountains
> was almost close enuf to grab the
> club
>
> then split down quiet street
> (*Dancing Bear,* [Berkeley: Undermine, 1969] p. [7])

In *Dancing Bear* the man-nature articulation is broken. Simon has been up in the mountains, has made his pilgrimage, but then returned, became politicized a la Krech:

> talking in sunlight
> 3000 feet above ventana canyon
> blue jeans over thorny flower
> started writing this weeks later, hungry
> 7 am, may 8, people's park
> (*Dancing Bear,* p. [1])

Even looking back on the "wilderness," Krech's memories are flooded with "man-presence"—12 gauge shotgun shells,

and stories about "some doctor" panicking in the first snow
and abandoning a 30.06 rifle and telescope lens, someone else
who was "high on pot or lsd or something" and thew away his
gear and wandered off into the snow:

> . . . . . had to shovel him
> into a sack to bring him home
> 6 weeks later
> (*Dancing Bear*, p. [3])

The union and communion are broken, and loneliness—the
time of purification in the "desert"—is turned into a night-
mare experience of "man-apparitions" intruding into the
purity of nature. Alone in a cabin in the mountains he imag-
ines a girl standing at the door . . . . only when she
approaches his bed instead of a face all he sees are "gray spider clamps," and then a stove pipe begins to "bang around in
the wind."

Man-man discord is transferred in Simon's mind to man-
nature discord, and no matter how far he tries to retreat into
"nature," to recapture the organic oneness he experienced
during his mystical initiations, this other man-man world
intrudes:

> far from here these bodies reflect light
>
> faces hands darting through open
>
> "cant catch me" thud of tooth on
> skull
> (*Dancing Bear*, p. [5])

As with Krech even drugs don't work any more. The
immediate political reality "out there" is too intrusively
strong. In *Roads to Dawn Lake* Simon prepared the drug-
based man-nature-union "revolution" ("at night smoked
hash, cinnamon, nutmeg, grass/the birds talk like black

leaves/we prepare change & revolution"), but now that the confrontation has come, passed and come again he finds himself totally "blocked," "cornered," "frustrated." When questioned about leading a bear (man-nature union) around, he hardly seems aware of it . . . . and is even less aware of the possibility of "dancing" with the bear—actually "celebrating" the permanent fusion of man-nature diversity:

> "what the hell would I be doing leading a bear"
> "thot you might dance with it"
> "dance with it"
> (*Dancing Bear*, p. [9])

Just as Simon's celebration of mystical man-nature unity represented the "fulfillment" of American "pro-spiritualism," his more recent work represents its present errosive standstill . . . . perhaps even its eventual "disintegration." Simon, like Levy or Krech or even Blazek, began in a state of radical innocence. The American begins as a "New Adam," unaware of evil, every new generation antedating the Fall. In *Dancing Bear* he finds a "dead moth in the/pages of lamentations" and comments:

> being american we were
> born without this knowledge.
> (*Dancing Bear*, p. [8])

Elsewhere he writes:

> "Innocence
> thats what it is"
> (*Dancing Bear*, p. [9])

The whole Hippie movement, beginning in the mid-sixties came to the scene proclaiming a new heaven-on-earth, a neo-humanistic doctrine of drug-based "charity" that would abolish war, institute a reign of peace and love, and catapult the human consciousness into a new dimension of expansive perceptiveness. Simon, Krech, the others, really expected hard-headed American industrial pragmatism to go Hindu and shimmer off into ragas of pure delight. Only instead, when the "movement" had reached what the Establishment considered a "danger point," when a kind of "spiritual takeover" seemed imminent, the reaction set in hard and violent.

For the poets, reality, instead of continuing to expand, suddenly stopped, held firm, converted from flowers, music, ecstasy, to "pig (cop) reality:"

> in a shadow of myself
> i pass through matching
> pigs boudoirs with barbed wire & crocodiles
> eating each other under the pale skin
> of a violet lagoon
> (*Dancing Bear*, p. [8])

Simon has an interesting book—pamphlet—called *The Adventures of the Floating Rabbi* (1968) which dadaistically burlesques the genuine quest described in *Roads to Dawn Lake*. There are eight chapters, and Chapter 8 is merely a black-page. Chapter 7 ("A Ski Race to Your Draft Board") reads:

> it ended on a snowy mountain. futile to recount the immense journeys which brought us here. we skiied downward in the fluid darkness thru thick trees. the last pitch was an empty hospital waitingroom. tilting downward and unlit. a cameraman posed all the racers as they came. afraid of his line of talk i said fuck it and descended while he was unprepared. sailing on thru the far door it turned out to be the draft board. appointments for the shrink, to save my ass once again, i took a seat between my dad and the hashish scarab.

The final rush here, of course, is to (Chapter 8) emptiness. But before emptiness there is the Establishment (draft board) to be faced, which Simon faces by compromising himself. He sits between his father (the "square world" of quest-departure) and "the hashish scarab" (the swinging early Krech-world of total psychic activation). And why? "To save my ass once again." The whole journey through "the kindly mesca-line chateau" (Chapter One, the initial drug-sensitivity initia-tion rites) the "Loosing the Venemous Arthropods" (Chapter Two, negative drug effects), the "Many Deaths and Reap-pearances" (Chapter Three, initiation through suffering), through "Underwater Near Hiroshima" (Chapter Four, the confrontation with "war"), the incident of "Fred the Schizo-phrenic" (Chapter Five, the danger of "splitting out" into psychosis), the "Breakfast Under the Mountain" (Chapter Six, a racial split in the drug-group), down to the final "Ski race to your draft Board" (Chapter 7) is a slow journey into total psychotic alienation. Chapter Eight represents Simon's psychotic anihilation of the "real" world. All meaning, direc-tion, "movement" are obliterated, and the "quest" ends in complete "dissociation" from all "real" and "theoretical" worlds. The entire drug-based enlightenment ends in the utter blankness of "psycheout."

Simon's dead-end conclusion to *The Adventures of the Floating Rabbi* applies very much to the latest developments and conclusions of the whole Hippy ("pro-spiritualist") movement, And perhaps this conclusion was as inevitable as Levy's suicide, because: 1) The industrial-technological milieu of the U.S. wasn't right for the development of a New Heaven on a New Earth, 2) The hippies themselves, like Simon, were NOT "detached" enough to allow themselves to—in the spirit of the Tao—cover "the ten thousand things like a garment" without making any "claim to be master over them."

Perhaps there is too much of the industrial-technological mystique in Simon to have ever allowed him to negate himself enough to move through the hard wall of American material-ism into the free-field of total selfness. In *Roads to Dawn Lake* Simon had written:

> they cannot learn
> nothing is to be said
> rightly.

On the other hand, though, perhaps the first journey has to end in blankness, because blankness represents a state of repose and recovery. Perhaps blankness is only one step in the overall quest and Simon, like Buddha in the frost, is undergoing the austerities of blankness (renunciation) before finally finding a new "middle way."

If Levy had survived perhaps he would have become a Buddha himself and Simon, still in his mid-twenties, might very well pass through his "trial" and become another Emerson, Thoreau . . . . another North American Buddha. Certainly this is the direction of the whole hippie quest movement, toward a full, rich and enlightened spirituality. It is too early at this point to be pessimistic about ultimate results. The finding of "God . . . . through heightened awareness of the world, increased commitment to the eternal in time," talked about in the *San Francisco Oracle* in 1968 (Vol. I, Number 12) as a kind of hippie "creed" has, in a way, been subverted by the political "coloring" added to what was an essentially apolitical, mystical cause. Simon, like Levy and Krech, was bombed out by being politicized, and he is honest enough to admit that politicalization can only end in a blank wall for a mystic. The question is now whether or not Simon—and "The Movement"—can be switched back to the problem of personal, interior growth . . . or really, perhaps, whether personal, interior growth is possible in the U.S. in the 1970's.

Joel Deutsch: A Process of Desensitizing

Joel Deutsch's earlier work is extremely soft, perceptive, delicate, a poetry made out of little things . . . little fears, little sensitivities, little uncertainties. He is very vulnerable, "undefended," permeable. He is love- and touch-centered, frankly and unashamedly confessional.

One poem in *Space Heaters* (1969) is particularly impressive in this "interiorized," small way, "Thank You for Your Kind Persistence/For Jane," perhaps the most acutely sensitive poem written by a U.S. poet in the last decade.

It begins in bed. Sleeping next to his wife, Deutsch finds himself separated from her by an immense distance he can't cover. Bed, distance, and then a sudden shift out of the bed onto the highway and a stalled car, trying to figure out what's wrong:

> tonight
> the several inches of bed
> between us
> were a distance
> i could not cover,
> like 400 miles of freeway
> with a bad engine
> & i'm standing there
> with the hood up
> scratching my skull

but i can't for the life of me
figure out
what it is that's broken

Not only is the car-marriage metaphor particularly apt, but the whole approach to the experience itself is very unusual for the underground. Instead of being existentially tough and playing big couldn't-care-less man, Deutsch opens the last door into his essential self, doesn't just confess painlessly and "formally," but mixes confession with a real sense of doubt. He doesn't have answers—and doesn't pretend he has.

Then, not stopping at this admission of personal "blocking" between himself and his wife, he moves into another very sensitive area: his own image of himself as a writer. He doesn't work, but stays home, cooks supper, cleans the house, while his wife works just so he can write. Only he doesn't write, but sits around paging through auto-parts catalogues:

oh, i've cooked supper
& cleaned the house
but it's hard & guilty
to greet you, home for work,
with my hands empty of poems
my mind consumed
by an auto-parts catalogue
& the bad taste of bile
where the words are stuck in my throat
like jammed typewriter keys

Here the whole range of reality has a very un-undergroundish focus. Deutsch isn't really outside the North American middle-class success-mystique. He isn't sitting on top of the American trash heap, roaming the American back alleys, in the shadows and basements—or in the mountains—of American reality. He's bourgeoise, playing the whole beat-hippy underground role straight, right from the middle of middle-class comfort—and he's unselfconscious enough about it to not turn it into a role.

"Thank You for Your Kind Persistence" ends with another powerful metaphor, an association-complex that links Deutsch's shame at not producing (itself a very middle-class value) with a motorcycle death he witnessed . . . which in turn is linked with the "raw meatness" of a pound of ground beef he was holding in his hands at the time:

> /it's how i felt
> when they pulled that man
> off his smashed cycle
> across the street
> & i stood by the market
> holding a pound of ground beef
> in both hands

All of Deutsch's early poems are full of this sense of "little-thing-ness," a concentration on the minute, the personal, the everyday—but always incorporating into this "smallness" a very large sense of tragic message.

In a poem like "New Shoes" (also in *Space Heaters*) Deutsch writes about a pair of old shoes still left around after he'd bought a pair of new shoes. He feels like throwing them away, "but they don't look/like they want to go." He would put them in the closet. They might even be fixed. But they want to stay around:

> i guess
> they got used to the smell
> of my feet
> & now they want
> to stay
>
> the way
> you get used
> to the world

In "Confusion of the Shy Dancer" this sense of disenchant-ment, of small, bitter "naturalism," expands, becomes historical . . . and myths begin to crumble:

> i know that curtains fade
> in sunlight
> i know that billy the kid
> was ugly & wyatt earp
> shot men in the back

For Deutsch the world is two-levelled, the surface level bland, harmless, even dull . . . while underneath this deceptive bland dullness the "essential" world is threateningly veined with "evil."

"The Renovation," for example, begins as a simple poem about sandblasting. A real estate company is trying to see if it is possible to renovate an old building, pretty it up, instead of tearing it down and building a new one. Only the renovation doesn't work, and the spectators who have been hanging around half-heartedly watching the attempted renovation haven't really wanted to see a renovation at all, but a total destruction. Which is what they eventually get:

> . . . . . pretty soon everyone
> cluttered the street
> with speculations & cigarette-butts
>
> until the wrecking machine
> rumbled in, swinging
> its single iron testicle
> & gave them
> what they really wanted.

Under the clothed, "regulated" surface, man the destroyer waits for, wants destruction. The message is strong, ominous. . . . and universally applicable.

And constantly applying this minute double-level reality-testing back to himself, Deutsch finds his own "appearance-reality" complex all full of the stress cracks of small deceptions:

I AM SO TIRED
OF BEING CONSUMED
BY MY GAMES
AND I AM SO TIRED
OF PRETENDING TO BE SOMEONE
I HAVE NOT BECOME
AND I AM SO TIRED
OF LOOKING ELSEWHERE
FOR MYSELF
WHEN I AM RIGHT HERE
IN THIS ROOM.
("Long Distance—for Susie")

This kind of "being tired," this self-search for someone who has already been found (or never really been left behind), though, is very deceptive in Deutsch's case because all of his early work is thoroughly self-aware. He has cut off from U.S. reality "out there" (both the PR and the Subterranean realities), cut off all outer communications and begun to communicate exclusively with himself. His complaint isn't really about a lack of self-knowledge, but his need to establish contact with the "out there," and giving into this need has, more than any other single factor in his development, turned him from a sensitive, very individualistic, "different" poet, into one of the "West Coast Gang."

Deutsch's more recent work is filled with the violently exaggerated metaphors, the forced, "energized" syntax-tearing, the tough-guy stances, the worked-over surrealism, that is common in the worst of Deutsch's new Poet-Master, Doug Blazek. What originally began with Blazek and Richmond as merely Meat Poetry has become a whole world-view, where everything that happens happens in hyperbolic comic-book fashion and time is broken up into little squares filled with pulsating, energy-haloed cosmic landscapes and peopled with much bigger-than-life super-heros. Here the delicately nuanced interiorizing of the early Deutsch (man on a trip "inside") is exteriorized, and the individual self-

probing replaced by a dynamics of overblown "thing-manip-
ulation:"

> the sun
>   spears itself
> bloody
>   on the mountains,
>   the roads
>   turn purple
>   at right angles
> & a neon sign
>   hums itself to sleep
> on the tallest building
>   in town
> ("Tucson Federal Savings—For Jane," manuscript poem)

Instead of just being at home and keeping the place clean,
preparing dinner, now reality moves into a whole new energy
dimension:

> i cook exploding stew
> in my bathysphere galley
> and sadly set the table
> for one. then your face
>
> appears in the porthole
> like one of those fishes
> that live in deep water
> and glow like market street
> on a friday night
> ("Electric Heartwarming," manuscript poem)

The "normal" reality here is a reality of "exploding
stew." It isn't stew that isn't supposed to
explode—"exploding" as a continuing fact is an integral part
of the psycho-engineering here. And rooms being too drab to
be taken merely as rooms are converted into bathyspheres
"submerged ten miles/beneath the twisted/fairytale
headlines/where the oakland stepmother/tortures her

baby/with a bunsen burner/and art linkletter/does a news-
print dance/on his dead daughter's grave."

In order to supercharge "ordinary" experience, at times
Deutsch slips into synaesthetics, driving sense-nails into the
poetic matrix one on top of the other:

> mexican girls
> rub crisp hair
> against the sheets,
> dreaming of dark men
>   to take them away
> *in chromed coaches*
>   *louder than christ*
> ("Tucson Federal Savings," my italics)

At times he dramatizes reality totally a la Western, mixes
up mythologies the size of theater marquee billboards. Like
his Michael McClurish "Gunfighter's Picnic," compounded
out of Hollywood and Billy the Kid:

> then the Kid moved, a gloved hand
> flashing in the fast eternity
> of the draw, & the killing
> was on. the sheriff
>
> put two slugs through the director's head.
> (Printed on a separate sheet as a "Lone Ranger
> Biology/Meatball Free Poem)

The poetry takes on the quality of TV ads, the rhythm very
nicely timed for dramatic effect ("all at once/the town came
out from hiding./a tablecloth to cover the bodies/& the snap
of beer-cans/opened in shady places"), the concentration
almost entirely on form, line, the click and ring of celluloid
drama.

In one poem, "Do you Come to Me, Love, From the Yellow Pages?", Deutsch merely sums up a series of telephone
book ads ("United Airlines/Western Auto Wreckers/Bay
City Coal Co," etc.), and then playing hard for shock-value

contrast fastens "the human touch" on the end:

> And your hand, warm
>   against my emptied balls
> Like none
>   of the above

The human remains, but it is electrified, "processed" now. Reality is no longer simple, low voltage, but full of Pop Culture wham, bash and bazazz. Somehow in his earlier poetry, Outsider Deutsch had avoided the "neonification" of reality. Nothing was Las Vegas sign size, but humped over, broken, human. In his latest work, publicity as a philosophical-poetic system* has taken over. The "product" has developed a kind of giantism, everything is much bigger than life-size . . . gestures, emotions, ideas, everything. Like in "Zip-Code—For Blaz," a description of listening to and gradually learning to appreciate Mahler. Three days nothing happens, and then on the third day:

> the garage-door of Heaven
> opened
> & God drove forth
> in a mint-condition Edsel
> to deliver his letters
> Himself!
> (In manuscript)

Here there is no more room left for implicitness or subtlty. Everything is forced out into the explicit openness and subtilties disappear under the weight of super-sell histrionics. The idea "I wonder if I could make love to you before dawn" in "Tucson Federal Savings" becomes "i wonder/could i race/the sun/to your soft door," in "Maypole Dance for the Grownups" (manuscript), the idea "the Hippies are trying to

*See Jules Henry, *Culture Against Man* (New York, 1963), Chapter III.

tell the consumption-centered public that consumption-values are worthless but the public won't listen" becomes: "voices come to him/from the catwalk./they tell him/it is all illusion./they tell him to stop struggling/but he can't see their faces./he flails his arms/and buys things." Sun-racing, soft-doors, flailing arms . . . we are thrust—very vigorously—into a whole new world of "over-write."

The Blazek-dominated Meat School is a particularly virile form of Neo-Naturalism, and like all Naturalism concentrates on the broadest possible delineation of life. Instead of being left unsaid, everything is over-said, over-stressed, over-burdened. The whole range of "interior" life is ignored for a concentration on basic, broad animal drives: sex-hunger, greed, hate, anger.

Even in his earlier poetry Deutsch is very "essential" in his poetic evaluation of human nature, but this "essentialness" is placed in an ambience of easily-triggered reactions to extremely low-keyed human needs. . . . the need for acceptance, the shame of not having "produced" or "performed" for a day, disillusion with the imperfection of the world around him. The big change is in the direction of eliminating the "small" need-reactions while at the same time double-stressing "essentialness." Basic, "brute" nature crowds out and overwhelms "totalness."

In the last pair of years Deutsch has moved from being a loner to a "joiner." He has come in from out of the cold and found group-acceptance rewarding enough to tempt him to leave behind his sensitivity and substitute "impact-writing" in its stead.

The Underground can have its own kind of conformity, and in an atmosphere of intense anti-Overgroundism peculiarly individual talents can be stifled. The Underground, especially now, as it becomes more and more organized, can provide an alternative success-ladder for highly motivated young writers. If you can't make it in *Atlantic*—which no longer even reads non-solicited manuscripts—you might be able to make it in *Open Skull*. Only to make it in *Open Skull* you have to write another kind of "party-line" poetry. If you have a non-conforming, out-of-it "different" self, this self has to be trained and twisted to fit into the non-commerical ("non-market") market place.

The only solution, of course, is to STAY out in the cold. But it's difficult, especially for a North American—trained to win, climb to the top of the pyramid, "make it big"—to detach himself entirely from "success." It is the same kind of problem that the younger hippy poets have had with detachment in general. They are not detached, floating mystics, but anti-establishment establishmentarians infected from birth with the need to compete and win, and to spend even a pair of years, much less a life, doing anything for its own sake, is just as heterodox in the Underground as in the Overground world. The Underground is an alternative—but still an *American* alternative, and subject to many of the same rules that apply to the Overground. Ideally the Underground should be kept "loose" and "undogmatized," but, as the case of Deutsch indicates, we are talking about a very real, not ideal, literary "clique." Still, there are a great number of other "cliques" in the Underground. . . . perhaps Deutsch will cut out, sample elsewhere, and hopefully either return to the approach he began with or find something even more individually his.

T. L. Kryss: Poet on the Run

T. L. Kryss is the most bone-bare, essential, existential, hard-knuckle, hard-core poet in the underground scene. He's *like* Blazek, but much more streamlined, less sentimental, less looming and baggy . . . . everything he writes is succinct, curt, almost telegraphic. He is the master of the "essential image." Take a poem that appeared in the magazine *Amper&and* (Mach, 1969) that Kryss edits in collaboration with R. Wolter. No title:

the rain
cripples
telephone
wires with
ice

a broken
baby carriage
covered with
a thin coat
of snow

a string of
light bulbs
glazed with
frozen
silver

a fender
bangs
against
the
bone . . . .

i put on
another shirt   ·

and listen
to the
baseball
scores from
arizona.

Also, like Blazek, Kryss' poetry often flows into surrealism, only in Kryss' hands surrealism isn't merely the coupling
of odd, unexpected and unusual images, but the juxtaposition
of normally unrelated images whose juxtaposition illuminates
and intensifies emotional impact:

my lips as illusory
as the skull of
a butterfly.
(from *Nuclear Roses & Quiet Rooms*, 1969).

Or in another poem talking about the wind that represents
the loneliness of the mob:

it is bounded on all sides by the echos of
                                        stars
it is the gentle wind that cleans the spiders
                            from my eyelids . . . .

Kryss' vision of reality is very similar to that of the more
recent Krech. He is very basically a social critic protesting
against the mind-sterilization that he sees behind the decline
and fall of the American dream. To Kryss the media gradually "processed" reality and created a pseudo-reality that
slowly became the only reality.

In a protest poem about the Viet Nam war he traces the whole deadening and paralysis of the American conscience to this media suffocation:

back home is where the war began
in front of the television
where death was a facile trick . . .
where love was restricted to movie sets
in the carpeted wasteland of flourescent libraries
where plastic words rattled in the overdue fine box
where the mind was burned with every dollar
                 squandered on new titles
& you could check out with ten tombs of wisdom
                 under your arm
& the prophets were kept under key . . . . .

it began
& is perpetuated by men
in whatever position of small authority
who spread the lie that words are magic,
that their words, in particular, are sancti-
fied by the nobility of their dreams
dreams borrowed, misinterpreted & stolen from
the grave,
                 dreams that will shape the death
             of america because
               there is no one left
               to shape his own dreams
from the dreamless steroid mass imagination
               no one left to dream
               new majicks
               write new newspapers
               destroy the column inch
               bring back the flowing
               circle.

Like many of the other living underground poets, Kryss is very much anti-media. The underground is very aware of the plastic transformation of U.S. society by means of media-manipulation. The "war" and the whole process of informa-tion-subversion began with editors playing "word games over private tables/in florida hotels." It began "with the newspa-pers that/brought the soul back into the/living room."—a synthetic soul, a carefully engineered and manipulated soul.

To underground poets like Kryss the whole modern scene is controlled by semantic-engineers. They are all painfully aware of the "real" reality. They vibrate to the rhythms of the contemporary world around them, the streets, the bars, the people, the ideas. And then they see this other "manipulated" world and realize that they, the poets, are the only ones look-ing at the "real" world, that everyone else is looking at the "manipulated" world and accepting it as the only, the "true" reality. For the underground poets the real enemy is this "dreamless steroid mass imagination," a kind of intentional, programmed reality that skips over anything "ugly" that admits guilt or blame and insists on presenting America and the American mind, the American conscience, as perfect, spotless, semi-divine.

This whole disillusion comes out in a poem on Detroit where Kryss goes through a long series of contrasts between the reality and the lie:

    detroit, do you
    make seatbelts
    out of black skins
    sewn together

    detroit, did you
    think you could
    wash yr bloody
    hands with gaso
    line, did you
    think you could
    hide yr murders
    in the glove
    compartment? . . . . .

detroit, henry ford
is mummified in a
bucket seat tomb
& wears a crown
of splintered
glass

For a while the "manipulated" reality worked: "....
(you) fed/yr people pictures/of the latest/model dreams
&/one meal a day &/built great gleaming/juke box factories
. . ." But it doesn't work any more: "detroit, blood/is leak-
ing out of/the bullet holes in/yr radiator."

This careful sensitizing of consciousness in the underground, of course, is merely one expression of a total split
right down the center of the North American world view.
Kryss' debunking is just one more version of a more general
awakening to the reality that doesn't appear on the TV, radio
or in the newspapers or magazines. The plasticized, homogen-
ized, sanitized mass-meda reality-picture is full of holes, and
the Blacks, the Mexicans and the Young are looking through
the holes at the world "as it is."

In 1968, Ghost Press in Cleveland published a volume
called simply "*For John R. Scott,* who painted flowers." In
1968 Scott was sentenced to two years imprisonment in
Warrensville Penitentiary (Ohio). Prefacing Kryss' poem is a
statement which very well expresses Kryss' whole attitude
toward reality versus appearance in American life:

> ". . . . . America is standing at the edge of its history,
> watching the action as if it were happening somewhere
> else."

This ability to watch the action "as if it were happening
somewhere else" is very much a part of the communications-
trap that the underground is rebelling against. "Processed
reality" turns the individual into an automatic spectator, and
by definition the spectator is "marginal," isolated from the

reality surrounding him. It is this psychic (spiritual) isolation that prevents the "public" from seeing what Kryss and the rest of the underground consider to be the gradual conversion of the U.S. into a police state.

Kryss in a poem similar to Bob Dylan's poem on the "hard rain" that's "gonna fall," writes about a rising wind "that crushes small animals/to the floor of the forest/. . . that . . . gathers in election squares of the world/(and) comes when the plastic radio/melts in my hands on the eve of the revolution." This wind is the "loneliness of the mob," and its very specific target is "The Electric Curtain." It "scratches/Mayan rubrics in the glass-eye of Radio Free/David Sarnoff" and is symbolic of a very specific case of general "mediaitis"—the media barrier ("the Electric Curtain") between the "people" and the "politicians."

Politicians have been "processed" like everyone and everything else, only the mob, marginal, on the processing border, sees through the processing to the reality underneath it, is disillusioned, angry, beginning to move:

> . . . it is the gentle wind that cleans the spiders
>   from my eyelids
> it is the wind that carries Caesars to my door
> i turn them away into the night with their
>   speeches in their hats
> and i listen to their footsteps in the wind/
>   the wind
> that only dead men do not hear.

Of course Kryss himself is beyond the marginal, a classic outsider, and his poetry is a classic example of the underground's ability to withstand "mediafication" and continue to maintain a sensitive and individualistic life-vision even in the face of massive standardization.

The undergrounder like Kryss resists "processing" by resisting incorporation into the processing system. Being neither the system nor the anti-system mob he retains the fresh vision of the pure spectator, isolated, unattached, moving by reality itself instead of imposing a system-structure on reality.

Kryss' poetry is filled with telegraphically curt reality-slices produced precisely by this kind of detachment, reality-slices that come as close to Blazek's ideal of "real-thing" poetry as anything else coming out of the underground. Blazek's Open Skull Press has published very few poets, and Kryss is among them. Kryss' pictures of "small realities" are among the best things he does—lying awake in bed at night with the chrysan-themum wallpaper "forming fear-flowers/in the dark," with a siamese kitten snuggling into his bed and licking the small of his back, watching the "cold profile" of the moon "against the dark sky/tangled in wet telephone wires," urinating into the sink, "the sound of piss splashing/against the porcelain," waiting for his woman to come home, "her orange cigarette flitting through the/darkness," passing a drugstore and seeing "small water toys in/the window that have/their own peculiar light of things/that have not changed positions/for a winter and a summer."

At the same time, though, Kryss inevitably adds another dimension to everything he does: mythic, allegorical, sym-bolic . . . . always finding patterns of much larger realities in the small things around him. And perhaps this ability to cap-ture the particular without losing sight of the general is the real finality of all "meat poetry," starting with the fragil, sensitive immediacy of the now and working out to a telling-it-like-it-is generalization.

The larger outlines of this "superstructure" in Kryss' poetry views the contemporary scene in terms of a kind of "industrial-military" invasion. The good earth, primal, Eden-like, innocent, has been tained by much more than mere media-processing—the "original," the "great" sin in Kryss' *mythos* is a destruction of the primitive.

In a poem called "Union Near Fleet" *(Amper&and,* March, 1969), for example, Kryss neatly contrasts the pre- and post-industrial eras by moving a bear (mythic innocence) through an industrialized wasteland:

    i watched a
    dying polar bear
    make tracks through
    the March streets
    and look away
    with disbelief into
    the night where
    he remembered . . . .

    the polar bear
    could not recognize
    the snow when
    it lay in the city . . . .

    he mentioned you
    might still be awake
    watching the
    northern lights through
    a hole in your
    blanket . . . .

    he told me
    that you no longer
    understood his silence
    and were living with
    an illusory snowman
    in a dark wounded
    room . . . . .

    i was speaking
    to myself when
    i told him
    worthless things
    about the city

    and the glass
    hotels i thought
    you died in
    on a clear chicago
    night marred
    with dreams
    of chalk.

Here the "you," the narrator—Kryss himself, or in a larger context Kryss' entire generation—has been cut off from mythic innocence, separated from the natural, and any contact he may have at all with the pre-industrial earth is filtered, partial, weak. He watches the "northern lights" through "a hole in (his) blanket" and can no longer understand "the silence" of the polar bear (the direct 'unprocessed' language of the pre- or non-industrial). He lives in the "dark wounded/room" of his "processed," anti-natural isolation and when he tries to establish contact with the natural ("i was speaking/to myself when/i told him/worthless things/about the city") he finds that the communication-channels are blocked both ways . . . . that "nature" cannot understand him any better than he can understand "nature." The city, the cumulative symbol of the anti-natural, is an insulating screen filtering out any communication from any "area" other than itself. It is closed back in and locked on itself and the "out there" has no possibility of pushing its way in."

At the same time Kryss recognizes that there is no way "back" for him. He can't return to the "natural" past ("i thought i might live there/in a stone windmill/and fish the bloodless river for/jade dragons/it was some mistake"), but is trapped in the world of the new, cancerous, destructive myths:

> . . . . thinking it is
> important to believe in some kind of
> myth, i glance out at the news
> papers rotting on the stone stairway,
> old men with brooms sweeping
> the mists out of door
>
> ways, spitting black phlegm
> on their showlaces
> and talking
>
> to themselves in soft
> puzzled tones.

The atomic bomb is "out there:"

> in oppenheimers desert
> a single dandelion
> gray and dusted life-force
> hangs its face in despair
> the passage of two decades
> has not changed the stillness

And what hasn't been sterilized by the bomb has been buried under mountains of industrial detritis: rusting freight trains, hills of coal, "phosphorescent foam/on the ohio/canal," trashcans, rundown hotels . . . all overshadowed by the threat of total media processing.

This depressed, despairing world-view is made even worse by the fact that Kryss traces the whole process of contemporary degeneration right back to man's basic nature. As he says in *Look at the Moon Then Wipe The Light from Your Eyes and Tell Me What You See* (1968) we are trapped in change, and to even imagine we can reverse our death-processes in a kind of ingenuous madness. A butterfly dies, a girl tries to breathe life back into it and fails:

> now everyone knows
> you cannot
> breathe life
> into de
> funct organ
> isms
> except this girl
> who was young
> and did not know
> about dead things
>
> she was crazy
>
> like a butterfly

Our limitations are ingrained in our natures: "the extent of your desire/may be traced in the length/of your finger . . . . your teeth are reliable clues/to your ability to survive."

Man simply because he is man is doomed. The old nature gods have been butchered and the new machine gods put in their places with harsh inevitability. Kryss ends *Look at the Moon* . . . . with a pro-animal, anti-human stand very similar to that of Whitman:

> peace on my planet to
> animals of no will.

Man wills, therefore he destroys, 'processes,' breaks down makes and re-makes, lets nothing the way it was . . . . in nature. Man is anti-natural because of his nature-dominating and destroying will, and when, in a poem like "San Francisco," he contemplates the destruction of an arch man-symbol, the city, he contemplates the post-man era takeover of the animals with relish:

> the golden gate bridge
> hovers weightlessly
> over the bay, flinging
> its final incentive in a bright
> steel yawn. i am waiting
> for the unwanted
> animals to pair off in silence.

Unlike most of the undergrounders, Kryss doesn't really believe in either the senses or "extended, expanded mind" (drug-culture) . . . . or even in revolution. The only really positive note, the only positive value he can hold up in an otherwise desolate psychic landscape, is his non-incorporation into the American psycho-physical machine world. The worst insult he can level at anyone is ("Tears, for Leslie Thompson & Jas. Veres"):

for you
the day
has become
a job.

Kryss stays resolutely "outside" the American mechanized junkworld. He has his soft, sometimes moments of sun and love ("the sun opens/in her fingers/after all these years/we feel the kiss/touch our minds"), but his trademark is his unbending dreariness, his rusted-eye view of industrial decline and decay.

He has his lyrical moments,* as in his poem about prison that appears in *Nuclear Roses & Quiet Rooms,* where there is an unexpected "want-personification" of the night in the middle of chains and cell rows ("what does the night want/does the night want a woman with warm blue breasts . . . . what does it want does it/want to cry on your shoulder"), but the jailhouse, rundown hotel, industrial warehouse and storage-yard, media-controlled world smothers any lightning-play of lyrical optimism.

Kryss' detachment is his greatest asset. Among the poets of the living underground he is the most accurate, poignant, condensed word-photographer. He is one of the great beggar-poets, far enough out of the Establishment to live within a constant panoramic overview of the contemporary scene in terms of its total inter-relationships and also its relationships to a dying, in many ways already dead, past, but far enough in not to degenerate into a mere harrangue or wail. Kryss is never the preacher, merely the recorder. He is the great click-record artist of contemporary transience.

---

*He and rjs did a book of folded paper experiments called *Dialogue in Blue* that is a lyrical masterpiece of visual poetry.

Richard Krech

Krech is the prototypical hippy of the Berkeley poets, with a huge, outspread bush of hair, (East) Indian flowered shirts, a love-child wife and a love-child child whose crying he never seems to notice, just ignores. He carries a kind of paradaisal insouisance around with him . . . . a radioactive field of "innocence," which recently has been changing into an increased political awareness.

His earlier work, *We Are on the Verge of Ecstasy* (1967), *How Easily Your Mind Can Slip Off* (1967) and *The Hashish Scarab* (1968) is almost exclusively concerned with "awareness." Krech is preeminently a pilgrim in the new drug-based quest into the fundamental nature of "knowing." "Ordinary," "normal" Richard Krech is surrounded by an unknowableness that the other "conditioned" or "treated" Richard Krech might begin to know:

> humans miss
> the high shrill sounds
> dogs respond to, we
>
> cannot know everything!
> *(How Easily Your Mind Can Slip Off)*

Like Leary and the other contemporary Northamerican psychonauts, Krech is really interested in reaching out, touching, knowing "the dancing molecules just beyond [his] . . . . reach."

He feels cut off from nature ("We have planted concrete/over the topsoil), isolated from social reality, cut off from really "knowing" reality around him by the inherent limitations of his knowing-mechanisms, turns to acid and begins to "exact" the inner nature out of things. He doesn't really penetrate "through" surfaces into "inner natures," but peels surfaces of reality and then concentrates on these isolated surfaces in their own uniqueness:

> the flat are of translucence
> floats lazily
> above my head.
>
> (in between my eye,
> & the external objects,
> i see things.
> > a film of cloth
> > draped
> > over the yes,
> or better
> > a layer of existence
> > stripped off
> > the objects.
> *(How Easily Your Mind Can Slip Off)*

All reality sharpens, intensifies, becomes highly energized and hopped up, reduced to its essential, molecular level. The energy in things comes out, begins to vibrate:

> i turn,
> > in the fresh summer air
> & walk up the street to my house.
> The Whole World Vibrating!
> *(How Easily Your Mind Can Slip Off.)*

Krech on one hand is simply "bored" by the flat, inane daily world that surrounds him. The level of everyday existence that he finds himself submerged in is the level that has been imposed on him by his past. It is the traditional, confining, harnassing world of his parents: "i walk down the center of the street,/deserted/of all forms of moving life." The center, middle-of-the-road tradition is dead, numb. But on the periphery there is always the promise of a fresh, generational renewal: "The green dawn/breaking/ above my head."

Krech never really stands still, but is always in movement, studying himself, seeing where he stands in relation to his own past, always avoiding stagnation, flowing, changing, adapting. Like Levy he wants to avoid categories and tradition-traps, poses or "fronts," but he is far enough away from being "caught," not to have to preoccupy himself with it the way Levy did. Krech is a free-floater. Never had been trapped, doesn't really know what a trap feels like.

Already in *How Easily Your Mind Can Slip Off* Krech showed himself aware of the historical dimension of the young Northamerican experience-seeker's predicament: "the kids/are hip, go places/their parents never dreamed of." His road toward reality is cut through (out of) the past.

Now in *The Hashish Scarab*, this "past" takes on a deeper, fuller significance. In *How Easily Your Mind Can Slip Off* Krech had obliquely blamed industrialization for the destruction of "natural" life, and in *The Hashish Scarab* the attack becomes more direct. In "Pome Against the Industrial Revolution," the real enemy begins to come into view. "Everything is/by definition,/natural," but the machine is less natural than non-machine nature. The machine and machine-thinking creates a new kind of non-human (anti- or non-natural) reality: "urban problems/are 'solved' on the/chemical & logistical level." Machine-thinking separates man from man-problems. Instead of adapting machines to fit "human rhythms," man adapts himself to fit "machine rhythms:"

> i just wonder
> if being 'natural'
> absolves the machines
>   originally

made by man
but after/awhile
he/begins/to/ad ap t/.

In *The Hashish Scarab* Krech's answer to industrial dehumanization is quite simply "pot." For Krech, pot represents a genuine escape route from the crippling boredom of the everyday. Routine is a spirit-crippler and destroys spiritual, psychic prescience. Pot gives psychic uplift ("our job is to stay high/above/the pedestrians") and protects the individual from anonymous, impersonal destruction, one of the basic characteristics of contemporary industrial civilization: "watch the shift crumble/from this vantage point/& you can't be hit/by falling objects."

Under the influence of pot all complicated, metaphysical, syllogistic reasoning is simplified to a heightened perception of the present . . . and then (one step further) through the physical wall of the present to the present's cryptic, usually hidden "inner" meaning: "We use things to try to get/beyond them."

The world as solid, static matter dissolves and speed takes it place:

the thunder
clapping its hands in time
with the blue silver lightning
from the clouds,

lights up our speeding world,
our car.

dissolving.
on this page.

Krech does not see himself alone in this vision of a pot-based paradise, but part of a movement, a whole world-wide psychic revolution. The Machine Age is being replaced by the Age of Pot. We are now merely in a transition era between the two ages, and the "pot seed/on the lawn/of the district/attorney" is merely one small sign of a much larger change. For Krech "the/long night is/almost/over," the long night of machine-centrism, of humanity subordinated "to the music/of I.B.M.,/the cymbals/of Teletype."

The meaning of the whole Hippy Movement for Krech is summed up in three lines:

> the street dancers
> appear to have won
>
> the next set.

The Flower Children, with their Love-Ins and Be-Ins, their "natural" hair and beards, their exotic, extravagant clothes that symbolized an attempt to actualize their inner selves to the utmost, in *The Hashish Scarab,* appear as an intermediate form between the Mechanical Businessman and the Drug-Based Guru. Peering far into the future, Krech even goes so far as to see the Pot-Generation as another transition form to a new type of mystic who puts aside even records, even the basic human obsession of preserving his past, and concentrating totally in the present. Savoring a bit of Isaac Assimov's Generation series, Krech projects into a different kind of human experience experienced by a different kind of human being, a human being humanized by drugs, relieved of his "obsessiveness," able to exist fully in the Now:

> after the legalization era
> there were several hundred years
> of enlightenment.
>
> however that is where
> the records leave
> off.
>   showing total
> pre-occupation
> with the
>
> present.

Recently Krech, still very much a representative of the young Hippy Mystique, has undergone a radical change. He has become politicized . . . . and the pot-based mysticism of *The Hashish Scarab* has given way to the far-left Maoist politics of *Mythology For the People's Liberation.*

The latest pamphlet I received from Krech was entitled simply *Berkeley Liberation Program.* It is unsigned, but many of the ideas in it coincide with ideas Krech has been supporting all along. Section 7, for example, "We Will Protect and Expand Our Drug Culture," is really little more than a militant, defiant prose version of *The Hashish Scarab:*

> We relate to the liberating potential of drugs for both the mind and the body politic. Drugs inspire us to new possibilities in life which can only be realized in revolutionary action. We intend to establish a drug distribution center and a marijuana cooperative. We recognize the right of people to use those drugs which are known from experience to be harmful. However, as a loving community we shall establish drug information centers and free clinics. We will resist the enforcement of all drug laws in our community. We will protect people from narcs and burn artists. All drug busts will be defined as political and we will develop all necessary defense for those arrested.

The Hashish Scarab existed in an unreal, apolitical world of personal experience extended to form an all-inclusive cultural theory. The *Berkeley Liberation Program,* on the other hand, is the dream of a hashish-paradise concretized and adapted to the real U.S. in the real twentieth century. It is an implementation of theory, a reduction of theoretical possibilities to actual probabilities.

The hippy movement, when it first sprang to the forefront of U.S. cultural life in the mid 1960's was—like Krech's early work—totally idealistic . . . . and unrealistic. It was supposed to literally re-form the whole psychic structure of the U.S. by introducing an overwhelming wave of "love" into American life. A child born in 1947 was 18 in 1965. Since

1940 the U.S. economy had been moving steadily toward increased affluence and by the mid-1950's a drastic change was being experienced in the whole "texture" of American life. U.S. culture had moved from survival-subsistence to luxury-experimentation, and the Hippy movement was a direct result of young people having more than enough money, more than enough time with more than enough "things" available to them. The environment had so drastically changed that a drastically new type of psycho-social orientation had resulted which believed that Utopia was here and now. The Hippies believed that the traditional essentially rigid, power-oriented, business- and work-permeated American mystique could be softened and transformed by their Utopian optimism. Only nothing changed, really, and the Viet Nam war, the assasination of President Kennedy, the Johnson and then the Nixon eras, edged the "official" American mystique back toward stiff traditionalism. The Utopians—among them Krech—found that the "establishment" wasn't giving way but, on the contrary, was moving against them. The "establishment" was not secure, but felt threatened by World Communism (especially Castro and Chairman Mao) on the outside, would like to have had a solid, traditional "Americanism" within the U.S., but instead was faced with a vociferous population of young people clamoring for "change"—change in the drug laws, change in the whole moral code of sexual relationships, change of clothes, change of hair and beard styles. . . . a desire for change that soon reached very specific target areas, among them the universities and the negro ghettos.

Simultaneous with the rise of the Hippies, the attitude of the blacks changed from that of Martin Luther King's patient "change through legal action" to "change through force." In the mid-sixties the cities and the universities exploded, and the by-words became Black Power, Hippy Power, Yippie Power. Impatient because they felt stalemated and paralyzed, the Young and the Blacks threatened the "establishment" with violence and the "establishment" reacted with more violence.

All these currents are very clear in the Berkeley Liberation Program pamphlet.

The attack is directly against the capitalistic power structure as such: "We will stop the defiling of the earth; our relation to nature will be guided by reason and beauty rather than profit. The civilization of concrete and plastic will be broken and natural things respected."

The radical black *and* white ideologies merge and fuse, and the whole apolitical love-philosophy that characterized the Hippies in the beginning is exchanged for a rather clear committment to world revolution:

13. WE WILL UNITE WITH OTHER MOVE-MENTS THROUGHOUT THE WORLD TO DESTROY THIS MOTHERFUCKING RACI-STCAPITALISTICIMPERIALIST SYSTEM.

Berkeley cannot be free until America is free. We will make the American revolution with the mass participation of all the oppressed and exploited people. We will actively support the 10-point program of the Black Panther Party in the black colony: all revolutionary organizing attempts among workers, women, students and youth; all Third World liberation movements. We will create an International Liberation School in Berkeley as a training center for revolutionaries.

This is a far cry from psychonaut culture of love and enlightenment preached by the early mystic-oriented Krech:

          our job
     is to stay high
     above
     the pedestrians,

> watch the shit crumble
> from this vantage point
> & you can't be hit
> by falling objects.
> *(The Hashish Scarab)*

In a poem that Krech submitted to a recent anthology, *The Living Underground,* he is quite explicit about his committment to violence and his renunciation of the old Zen-Drug way to enlightenment:

> i keep the gun
> on top of the books
> in the corner by the radio-active telephone
> the f.b.i. man
> walking around the house
> in circles.
>
> this is not a methedrine poem.
> i do not deal with the unreal.

Krech is still in his early twenties. He is one of the few writers who have been able to switch into writing revolutionary poetry without losing his force, succintness, clean, hard style. Too much "revolutionary" poetry is flaccid and unreal like Diane di Prima's *Revolutionary Letters:*

> are you prepared
> to hide someone in your home indefinitely
> say, two to six weeks, you going out
> for food, etc., so he never
> hits the street. . . . . . .

Of course Diane di Prima is a Beat-converted-into-Hippy. When she reads she lets her hair out loose into a wirey mane, when she finishes she ties it back very neatly—all the time lashing out against electricity and modern transportation . . . . after having arrived by car and standing on a stage talking through a P.A. system while bathed in bright light.

Krech is much more the "real thing." He has always played it close to the real line, no frauds, no tricks, no stocks and bonds up his sleeves . . . which is perhaps the reason why he has been able to make the transition from drug- to revolution-poet.

Once D.A. Levy wrote:

> . . . . . really i dont
> want to burn buildings or start
> a revolution
> (the revolution is inevitable)
> & i dont want to be here when
> is starts . . . . .
> (from the front page of *The Buddist*
> *Oracle,* 2nd Last Issue, November, 1968)

Levy represented the total, complete Hippy pacifist: frustrated, alienated, often angry, but disconnected from any larger, socio-economic orientated involvement. Krech, on the other hand, represents the post-Levy generation, the "involved poet." Levy's stance is already disappearing, Krech's is very much the stance, the belief, the committment of NOW.

Richard Morris: Squaring the Circle

One of the outstanding characteristics of the current U.S. underground poets is their total frankness. They make a point of being "confessional," without secrets or shame, attempting to get rid of all traces of self- or social-deception. For them total openness is equatable with self-knowledge *and* social acceptance. Acceptance begins inside; the Ego, Super-Ego and the Id all make friends with each other. . . . the "consciousness" recognizes the legitimacy of all its unconscious flora and fauna. And once the individual has made friends with himself he becomes part of a larger "new wave" of psychological self-acceptors.

Richard Morris, especially in his early work, differs from most of the underground in the fact that he is not confessional, but "controlled." He screens and filters out much of his real, subterranean self, and the poems that emerge are very similar to overground poetry that differs from the underground precisely in being "constructed" instead of jaggedly and emotionally "felt."

In his 1967 volume, *He Dreamed,* for example, Morris even uses techniques akin to Dick Higgins' "aleatics" in his "Joyous Collage Praising Abstract Expressionism," a poem that "incorporates statements about art by William Baziotes, Willem de Kooning, Arshile Gorky, Adolph Gottlieb," and other critics and painters. Another poem in the same vol-

ume is concocted "With Borrowings from Günter Grass."
In *Camels Coming* Number 7 (1967), Morris' own magazine, he wrote a review of Blazek's *Ole* #7 in which he more or
less "places himself" in relation to the whole new underground tradition. *Ole* #7 was a huge 112 page issue of critical
reviews written by poets like Bukowski, Wagner, Blazek,
Levy, Brown Miller and myself. I remember Blazek's only
restriction on me, when he asked me to contribute to the
issue, was to "be honest, don't be phonily polite." The overall
effect of *Ole* #7 was to create a more or less unified theoreti-
cal-critical attack on the "Poetic Establishment." As Morris
says, *Ole* #7 turned out to be "a manifesto directed against
the poetic tradition associated with William Carlos Williams,
Charles Olson, Robert Creeley, and others." What do the
new poets want?

> . . . . . a poetry that is 'more alive'; that is, less intellec-
> tual, containing more direct relevance to their lives.

The recurrent theme, as Morris points out, is "that too
much intellectualizing kills poetry, that a poem must first
have direct emotional appeal."
Morris' own reaction to this *Ole* manifesto reveals a great
deal about his own "mid-way position" between the howling
barbarian underground and the whispering, simpering overground:

> Like that of all revolutionaries, their propaganda is one-
> sided. These poets cannot see their opponents' virtues or
> their own faults. They too often forget that a poem can be
> quiet, yet powerful; and they tend to confuse the shock
> value of some of their own poems with genuine emo-
> tional content. They want poetry that is 'direct.' As a
> result they often distrust poems that are difficult.

From this it might be expected that Morris' own poetry
would be quietly powerful, understated, "difficult"—and
certainly his early work tends to go in these directions,

although only recently has he begun to be what can be really termed "difficult." His earlier work is really more "sweet" and "sentimental" than anything else, almost like D. r. Wagner when he'd tried to play pre-Fall Adam:

The poet is drunk.
Dreams grow,
and pain towers
above his eyes,
beyond his sight;
the poet is drunk,
the morning star is bright.
(untitled, in *He Dreamed,* published as *Quack,* No. 2, Reno, Nevada, 1967).

This dreaming, romantic Morris, unlike most of the microscopically "factual" undergrounders, begins mentally and then works out toward the outside world. He is not a "recorder," but a "planner," a visionary. What really distinguishes the underground from the overground is their reportorial confrontation with total reality. They do not selectively filter out distasteful, negative elements, but include the total reality-spectrum. The early Morris, on the other hand, still very much linked to "romantic overgroundism," moves through the contemporary scene subtracting ugliness and generalizing facts into easy-to-live-with idealistically-colored wishful-thinking:

Wind blows sand into flowers.
Then rain falls,
and dreams tower
above the clouds
above the rain
above the flowers
above the pain.

In the midst of all this romantic unrealism, though, Morris does manage to set down the one theme, the overriding emo-

tion that runs through most of his work, varied and transformed in different contexts and purposes—the theme of
alienation.

Once Morris finally drops his wishful thinking, he becomes
preeminently the poet of aloneness, detached loner in the
lonely crowd. The statement about loneliness in *He Dreamed*
comes through the romantic matrix like a bone splinter stick-
ing through skin:

> I walk.
> It is a long way to death.
> I am alone
> with my hands and a dying
> wind, bone, and my breath.

Between his early derivative, basically non-underground
romanticism and the very underground, very sensitively-
aware-of-the-scene-around-him present work, Morris went
through a middle period of simplification . . . . and purification.

In *Prey* (1968), for example, Morris arrives at a very neatly
honed-down, fragmented dramatization of his early outcry
about loneliness. Flat statement has been converted into a
drama involving "things" moving:

>   my eye follows
> a street/
> in the
>   distance
>   forms move
>   my eyes   rest
>   it has no
> end
> ("In the Air There are Echoes," *Prey,* Portland, Oregon:
> Wine Press, 1968.

Abstraction becomes total "thingness," and sometimes
Morris himself isn't involved at all. Like Larry Eigner he

forces "things" to express their own "innerness," revealing their "separateness." We aren't in a unified, organic universe but rather split off into separate, unrelated compartments. Any kind of "oneness-with-the-universe" is an illusory pattern imposed by alienated man whose sanity depends on some identification between himself and cosmic patterns. But still the patterns in themselves don't exist, we are in a happenstance cosmos of pure indeterminacy:

```
                                  a silver
          banner

          crack:
  a white    moving    twig
                          chrome
  on the
     freeway
  ("The Branch")
```

Morris has a Ph.D. in Nuclear Physics, although he doesn't work as a physicist, but as San Francisco-based secretary of COSMEP, the Cooperative of Small Magazine Editors and Publishers. His nuclear physical world-view comes through in *Prey*. The personal lamentations of Richard Morris, romantic, give way to the impersonal, objective observations of Richard Morris, scientific realist. There may be "much sorrow in the world," but the world isn't listening to man and man isn't listening to the world—merely trying subjectively, very desperately to survive:

```
     But the wind will not listen.
     And I will not understand:
     but live
                    only.
```

In *Prey* Morris refuses to inject himself into reality in any way and in the poem "To a German Poet"—unnamed,

perhaps Grass?—he complains about the poet's "dark puns"
which are:

> lost to my brittle
> conscious, my only literal
>
> mind
> or sense

Interestingly enough, though, Morris' literalness in *Prey* is
extremely "selective." He has gotten rid of the overgroun-
der's romantic impermeability to "thingness," but at the
same time has limited himself to a very narrow range of
things, very little more, really, than the reality of the cover
photo—a man silhouetted against a cumulous-cloud-choked
sky, a part of a broken fence, some reeds in the right fore-
ground. What's missing is Blazek's factories and Kryss' rundown hotels, Krech's "poet," Wagner's dirty sex. Like
Simon, Morris concerns himself solely with "nature," but
unlike Simon there is no quest involved, merely disunity,
separation, "hurt." If anything, nature is "predatory" like
the "White Birds Black Against a Whitened Sky" of the title
poem. To Morris the predatory cruelty in the world is "massive:"

> winds and fall,
> beginning: death. this
> one; and that death.
> a world, a head
> emptied, became remote, it,
> winging, was predatory
> and slight.

Nature outside of man is charged with the "massiveness of
prey," but man-nature ("a head/emptied") caught up in the
mechanisms of world-death, is himself merely predatory in a
slight, insignificant degree. The only link, really, between
man and nature is death.

Don Giovanni Meets the Lone Ranger (1968) in a way represents a reaction against the emotional "involvement" in *Prey.* The poems in *Prey* aren't safe, but walk the lunatic edge between "control" and "psychosis." The world presses in cruelly on Morris' consciousness but instead of defending himself against the punishment of amplified awareness he accepts it: "I/talk wounds, they/make/blood around my skull." ("Faces.")
Don Giovanni Meets the Lone Ranger is much more consciously "controlled." Morris holds back. Form takes precedence over emotion and content. There are many similarities to George Hitchcock's very urbane, ironic, stiff-lipped imagistic surrealism:

> I was drinking tea
> in a coffeehouse
> when
> in
> flew a virgin
> bearing roses.

Dramatization is abandoned, the poet removed from his subject and the world it represents. "Thingness" takes over and the whole poetic "purpose" and "vision" is limited to small, reduced thing-facts:

> a jug
>   of wine
> I broke
> a jug
>   of wine
> busted, running
>   over
> the floor.

At the same time, however, *Don Giovanni* is a burlesque of Morris' own poetic limitations. Every line, every word in *Don Giovanni* is charged with a dual sense of seriousness and self-mockery. At last Morris faces himself and the limitations of his stylistic allegiances, limits himself to working within the boundaries of the Williams-Olson-Creeley "schools," forces as much as he can of reality into the limits and strictures of these boundaries, all the time quite aware that the baggy unboundaried nature of all-reality is severely truncated and disfigured by this kind of forcing.

Morris' "cruelest" poem, cruel to both himself and his sources—his leanings toward the Overground instead of the Underground—ridicules Robert Creeley's well-made, perhaps "over-made" poetry, and points up the fact that the Creeley approach must necessarily always be "formal," "structural," "dead:"

> I saw two crows
> fat crows
> perching
>
> Two crows
> sitting in a tree
> I think (he sd)
> one laughed at me
> An end (he sd)
> is the thing we desire
>
> Crows are black canaries
> Crows sing
> ("The Conspiracy," For Creeley & the Crow in his Dining
> Room *Don Giovanni Meets the Lone Ranger.* Cleveland, Ohio: Posit Ion Press, 1968).

Not only is this kind of "reality" overly self involved with sound and word-on-the-page relationships, but it eventually becomes "cute" and even "coy" in extending the real out into sur-real distortions—crows becoming singing black canaries. Besides, Creelian reality is unacceptably divorced from the "movement," the whole wave of new mystical socio-economic consciousness and change that Morris is in many ways personally committed to. Morris first looks at it as well-made poetry made in a social vaccum, then twists the question around and asks. . . . is it even well made?

More recently Morris' work has undergone a striking shift away from academic "formalism" to a much more free-wheeling, more reality-inclusive approach.

Currently he is working on a poem called *Greyhound Bus Poem* which completely leaves the academy behind, cuts loose, and in a Kerouacian frenzy starts moving across the retina of total U.S. socio-economic reality. The "reality package" is complete: the old man "who looked like Karl Marx . . . . waving a sign . . . . 'COME TO JESUS THROUGH THE HOLY SPIRIT,' " the drunken cowboys in the back of the bus giving each other blow jobs, the babies crying, the inane conversations, the violence. . . . all "accepted" with wry irony as a normal part of the sociological landscape.

Buses have become a real obsession for Morris—because he has cut himself loose from tradition as a poet, and from any routine in his daily life, because he has begun to approach life experimentally, accepting "experience-forms" that are imposed on him from outside, instead of trying to force the world around him into a stiff, mirror-image of his own interior mind-structure. Morris has become "permeable"—the ion-flow of give-and-take-reality is fast and active. . . . and, of course, the greyhound bus not only cuts through all American reality as it moves across the country, it in itself is a symbol of the failure of the pioneer spirit, the breakdown of the New Jerusalem pilgrim impulse, the whole sense of human loneliness lost in an endless night of humming technology:

> This Greyhound
> local has already
> stopped at Shurz, Pocahontas,
> Jesup, Dermott, Quincy,
> and Hope. During the last
> hour it has not gotten
> nearer its
> destination.

Some Greyhound
buses are ghost ships
filled with gaunt
souls who stare vacantly
out
the windows.
("Greyhound Bus Poem," in manuscript. To be issued in
*Ginsburg Smoked Some Dope and Einstein Played His
Violin.* East Lansing, Michigan: Ghost Dance
Press, 1970.

As Morris becomes more and more people-oriented, more
and more interested in the punctured and dying everydayness
of the American "zeitgeist," his poetry becomes increasingly
tragic and "hurt-charged." When he applies his physicist's
time-perspectives to this everydayness, a delicate sense of
tenuous fragility comes through. Human-time condenses
down to an abrupt minuteness, a dry snap of the fingers, a
sudden curt emergence into and withdrawal from light:

Sometimes, in the grey light, I watch as they
climb on buses, or put
up billboards, as they
look in store windows or up at
airplanes. Sometimes I
watch as one comes suddenly
out of his black night and stands
for seconds in the
neon brilliance.
(Untitled manuscript poem)

When he talks about the "five species/of rhinocerous,
all/nearly extinct" ("Happiness is a Pet Unicorn," manuscript) he is really talking about mankind.

Morris has returned to his "loner in the lonely crowd" role
only with a heightened awareness that this loneliness is as
much a part of "humanness" as skin and old age. Loneliness
for him no longer consists in the artful fragmentation of
mass-reality; nor does he feel it should necessarily be an "out-

cry," but rather fact, an empirical statement on the human condition:

> We talk and nothing speaks: black
> holes our mouths. Air is caught
> by teeth in traps. Ears hear them
> close. . . . . .
> (Untitled manuscript poem)

Like Simon, Kryss, Krech, Morris wants to go beyond words. The best, perhaps the only communication, is touch ("the mind leaping,/ear closing, eye touching, hands/coalescing."), but at the same time he feels that too much closeness crushes perception, and backing off from reality to study it for a mute, existentially brief moment, it suddenly "reveals" itself, exposes all of the paradoxical, unexpected roots and fragments that were hidden inside it:

> love,
> the ocean
> remained bare when I
> worked at the branch, the ground
> was littered with words:
> backing
> off. I saw smoke
> in your hair
> like a tiger and oranges
> (Untitled manuscript poem)

Never expecting either human- or thing-reality to surrender its innerness to him, Morris contents himself with the small explosions of "contact" and "unity" that drift between him and his surroundings. In a poem, "For Sharon," he captures Sharon Asselin's technique of total despairing surrender to the tactile moment of "oneness." Loneliness breaks, we are instantaneously united in need, and then fall back into the vacuity of our aloneness:

> light
> brown, your

eyes, the ways
they light

on things,
the way your

mind goes,
love, touching

me
      (touching

The dominant emotion in Morris' more recent work is one
of filagreed nostalgia—the lonely busride across a lonely
country, the breakdown of communication, enclosing us all in
our own skin, coming together for fragmented moments of
touch-unity . . . . only one thing really seems to terrify him:
the gradual invasion and takeover of "artificialness." He uses
Reno, Nevada, as a catchall symbol for this "force," the same
"force" that is essentially feared by all the undergrounders,
the takeover of Fromm's "Megamachine:"

> In Reno, Nevada the old ladies play slot
>   machines and never stop.
> Reno, Nevada has an efficient police force,
>   an annual rodeo and an active Chamber
> of Commerce.
> Reno, Nevada was named after a Paiute Indian
>   chief called Reno, Nevada.
> General U.S. Grant wanted to be buried
>   in Reno, Nevada.
> Guiseppe Verdi wrote an opera called "Reno
>   Nevada."
> When Jesus Christ was nailed to the cross,
>   he cried out, "Reno, Nevada!"
>
> Sometimes I awake suddenly from fearful
>   dreams: like some huge beast, Reno,
>   Nevada is crawling toward me across
> the desert.
> ("Reno, Nevada," manuscript poem)

Here as in his recent bus poems, Morris shows a whole new cultural-historical dimension to his thinking. The "out there" becomes massively menacing. He has become an undergrounder participating in the healthy anxieties and paranoia of the underground consciousness necessarily sensitive to the changes in the structure and texture of the society around him.

Morris represents the positive influence that "the Movement" can have on a basically "straight" poet. Beginning well within the square Williams-Olson-Creeley tradition that avoids all and any variety of "human discharge" (either inter- or intra-personal), Morris has gradually allowed himself to come into the open, under the skies of the American dilemma. The defensive stiffness is gone, and he has relaxed into the kind of give and take human which may be the best product that will eventually come out of the Hippie Revolt. Morris, without flipping out entirely and falling over the psychout edge, has become a *guru,* perceptive, balanced, altruistic . . . . affectively flexible in the midst of U.S. production-consumption inflexibility. And isn't the whole purpose of the whole neo-tribal revolution precisely that—to produce *gurus?*

Charles Potts:
Died and Reborn Laffing Water, Full-Time Guru

Laffing Water (Charlie Potts) is the most sophisticated and at the same time most genuinely spontaneous poet-guru on the current underground scene. His language more than anything else reveals the "background" that pours into him as he freaks out and prophecizes. Not "rain," but "dravidian rain," not "with backbone," but "in the spirit of chordata," not "dust in my mouth," but "in my stomata," all very functional diction that in *Blues from Thurston County* (1966), for example, ties man even semantically into the whole of planetary life.

Laffing Water thinks in planetary terms. He comes into poetry with an ecological sense of order and "the natural," with a weight of scientific knowledge that he carries lightly enough to mix with direct, ingenuous, painfully open personal revelations. But Laffing Water, the visionary, the prophet, the guru, comes on chanting more authoritatively, more "convincingly" than other gurus on the scene, because the reference points of his visions are both intimately personal and objectively "scientific."

Like many other contemporary U.S. poets, Laffing Water is eschatological ("the abyss is moving foreward"), but unlike them he does have answers, and is filled with a sense of his own prophetic divinity:

once at the nadir
i went divine
instead of mad
(*Blues from Thurston County,* Part 6)

or,

im so mutherfucking devine
i sit on gods rite hand
im he who am who is . . .

ive got an answer for everything
even faintly resembling
authority and control
must be destroyed
immediately

and one question
for everybody

are u with me
or against me
("The Nitty Gritty," *Little Lord Shiva,* Berkeley: Noh
Directions Press, 1969)

This Christlike sense of "rightness" gives Laffing Water's whole life and work greater "definition" and power than his peers. When you are with him you feel in the presence of a truth-bearer. Balding, bearded, wearing moccasins, amulets, loose, shaggy, baggy clothes, his image is "him," not copied but secreted from inside. He doesn't flip back and forth between hate and love, wearing Zen like a coat that he puts on and takes off according to the weather (and audience), but maintains a steady, cool radiance, the radiance of a mystic who's "in" and no longer has to make a great effort to stay there.

The "message" that comes through from guru Laffing Water is clear and simple—*Be Natural, Love Thyself and Thy Neighbor!* In the Snyder-Simon tradition, Laffing Water bases all psychic explorations on the flesh, extrapolat-

ing out from the flesh into other regions only after the flesh
has been thoroughly savored, "exhausted," enjoyed:

> what is love
> is not this functure
> where everythings warm and wet
> and chewing on each others flesh. . . .
> i can smell u days after
> ure gone
>
> love wont wash off
> my bebe
> my body is absolutely certain
> and we slept the dead sleep
> having fucked out and off
> all our fears
> and circle in the afternoon
> around a dreamless sleep
> ("Feedback," *Little Lord Shiva*)

Nature flowers and floods through his mind automatically. In a sense he is an automatic (always-high) "see-er"
who doesn't select word-idea complexes for presentation, but
allows thought to "flow" out of him.

One of the great beauties in Laffing Water's work is the
poignant delicacy of these "flows" whenever they touch
nature—his fragile human flesh pressed by the "out there."
In section 8 of "Uproar and Feedback" (in *Little Lord
Shiva*), for example, he begins with a commentary on the
coming apocalypse, the survival of the "nimble and the
sleek," moves through a striking paen to those who "dug the
dirt/and swam thru water/and planted the seeds/and made
the bread/and loved the bed," switches over to a totally
unexpected presentation of an actual experience of himself
as nature-, life-, and body-lover:

> . . . .we went together
> nothing but darkness
> nothing like a bottom less

```
    pit with the sound of water
    off point lobos
    and i ran out on the tide
    pool
    to see if i cld tell
    where it drained
    and they said
    u were lucky
    and i said no
    i cld see the wave
    and yes i hurried
    and it was slick
    but i saw it coming
    and got out of the way
    and continued my rap down
    of the sea lions
```

    ARGHK   ARGHK

    ARGHK   ARGHK

Here he moves into and splices, actually "merges" with nature. He could have been "caught" by the wave, others ("they"—the non-mergers) are afraid for him, but he sees, hurries, escapes, continues as an integral part of the nature-totality, guru and sea-lions merely two similar variables of the same basic reality-expression.

This acceptance of his "natural," organically-united self is further accentuated in this same passage by following the sea-lion episode with a section where he is told (in a dream) that he has diabetes.

His reaction is typical of his overall "naturalness." Things will function "naturally" or they won't function at all:

```
    i will eat what food i like
    and sleep with whom and whom
    i please
    and life goes on
```

Laffing Water's "naturalness," though, is hard-won.

Charlie Potts, the "petit bourgeoise" who was motivated to "get an education" and make it, own two cars, "do well" had to kill his middle-class self in order to complete the "cycle" be reborn as a bonified guru, then as a guru re-make himself to fit his "necessary" (inner-directed) image:

> charlie potts is dead. . . .
> my name is laffing water
> and whatever form it takes
> i have plenty of
>
> changes to go thru
> before i outrite
> all my errors
> ("Fu Hexagram 24 No Hangups," *Little Lord Shiva*)

In spite of his second birth, however, Laffing Water still feels a lot of the past hanging on. He doesn't even necessarily dig his own language ("I feel trapped/with so many other ugly americans/locked in english"), which accounts to a great extent for his constant phonetic, "u" instead of "you," "yr" instead of "your," no capitals, always a small "i" instead of "I." "The dead [embrace] the living," he complains, and begs "let go of me."

A lot of the autobiographical comes through in Laffing Water's poetry, the girls he didn't "make," his mother, his favorite breakfast of pork chops with biscuits and gravy, the farm he grew up on; but he offhandedly rejects most of his past because of its bourgeoise restrictiveness, and only allows it to serve as a kind of emblem or leitmotiv of his central "nature"-preoccupation.

In a sense Laffing Water is a nature-fatalist, doesn't believe in anything fixed, but considers that he—as part of the biosphere—must necessarily disappear, be replaced, lose his individuality in cosmic massiveness. As he allows his past to filter into his present in "Uproar and Feedback," for example, even the "good"—non-bourgeoise—past is ground up in the cosmic destruction-machine:

and life goes on
and i get off
a few good rocks
before retiring
to cry my empty heart
with tears for the baby boy
as he stood arms around
the telephone pole
at the halliday underpass
has been replaced
with the benton overpass
and the pocatella house came down
when they cut the trees along the river
to prepare for a flood
and all my old friends have gone
on their own wobbling trips. . . .

Past "things" flow and flood through his mind. His only coherence is very free association, and within the anti-system system of this association everything is dissolved in flux and change. The species, of course (the "whole"), survives, but the individual is swept up in natural "processes" that really take little account of his individuality:

before the beginning
was nature
after the end
will be nature
                    never ending
now im on yr side
'nothing gets closer'
its like being hi
all the time
as my life approaches
the floating zone
kayos is verb
and everything moves
to the unchanging standard

nature
    keep spinning
gas into stars
to shine for me
when my lite
is gone
("Tantrum," *Little Lord Shiva*)

Laffing Water's "entrance" into cosmic oneness, of
course, is through drugs. He is a drug-based contemporary
psychonaut who has totally flipped out and away from
linear, non-visionary occidental squareness into curved,
ecstatic non-occidental simultaneity, mixes beer, "marko
pete" and methedrine in a courageously casual plunge into
organic cosmic anonymity. Not waiting for his light to go
out, in a sense he snuffs it out himself periodically (that
"light" that represents sequential, logical awareness) in
order to approximate that unchanging standard that fills the
life of organic and non-organic nature.

Death in any form never frightens him because he sees
that individuality (individual consciousness) is a barrier
between his real, inner self and the overall, universal "out
there."

For Laffing Water "real" death is unrelated to exploded,
expanded consciousness, is a function of bourgeoise mind-
shrinkage rather than drug-expansion. As he says in "A Little Birdie Told Me:"

    ikarus didnt die
    that is a greek mistake
    its impossible to get
    too close to the sun

Habitually linked to a large scientific world-vision, Laffing Water places him and his fellow mind-expanders at the
end of a long evolutionary development that moved to (then
through) logic into intuition:

> . . . .ego doesnt matter
> cus were at the end
> of the progressive uptite
> that produced the human head
> and i banish fear with love
> and the other rules
> the nite
> when dry heaves of love and gass
> come singing
> off the great cloud of magellan
> and the tarantula nebuli
> ("Uproar and Feedback" *Little Lord Shiva*)

Drugs and love (drug-induced love) initiate a Whitman-esque cosmic inclusiveness. He gives his "ego" (the great evil-source) up to merge and dissolve in a love-union which in turn merges with the larger, cosmic actions and reactions. The cosmos descends and he (love-spliced) ascends to meet it and become one with it.

Love, however, is the necessary beginning for all "flights." We are trapped on earth in slowly dribbling-out sequential time until "we surround/ourselves with each/other/and transcend the bloody whining/about life and death/those half nouns of/the dark and lite." Then, once the love-union has begun, we begin a trip really beyond life and death, reconciling the opposing yin-yang forces around and within us that have split us schizophrenically down the middle. The ultimate "trip" is the love-trip, the "us"-trip, and our ultimate reality is ourselves. We are our own life and death, our own heaven or hell. How we behave, whether we really make it into "unity" or not, determines the whole content of our knowing and being. When our heads come "whole" and cease to concern themselves "with trips other than ours" then we have traversed the whole universe of change and returned to our own sane beginnings. We reside and thrive within our-"selves," and our insane fears about death (or life—as a theoretical proposition) all disappear as we reenter our animality and we make our world exclusively "warm and wet."

Laffing Water's ecological vision always seems to slide back to "the nature of things" in such a way that man's splitting off from "nature" into separate, studied, contrived "civilization" comes out as the original sin. He submits to the true laws and rules of his nature ("I am basically/an alimentary tract/open at both ends/and cared for by a chemistry/far beyond/my ability to breakdown/and create.") and then once this has been taken care of he rolls with the rhythms around him, doesn't rebel against, but cooperates with his own inner love (and "expression") needs:

> and i want only to sing
> with my fingers moving
> across the guitar
> fretless and pleased
> with the nature of things.
> ("The 2nd Coming of Joseph Smith" *Little Lord Shiva*)

Laffing Water is one of the rare gurus who have really "made it." He represents, ideally, what the rest of the guru-hip poets are striving for and very seldom reach. His poetry and life fuse and shine together. He is what he says he should be. He has tripped out and returned in one damaged but still functional—and very resplendent—piece. He convincingly preaches that life should be love-centered, that expression should be inner-based and otherwise directionless, that we should be like sea-lions or birds or eskimos, that our civilization and our goals shouldn't be separated from either our inner blood- and gene-based natures, nor the cosmos stretching out around us.

Even "high" stylistically, he writes from a kind of fourth inner dimension where external time stops and everything is always clear.* His own past, the sweep and curve of "na-

*See "Free," in *Little Lord Shiva.*

ture" around him, the extension of cosmic space around his earth-world, all come together inside him where he hasn't really dropped "out," but "in." Laffing Water's message to us is to love, "let the spirit/lift up yr clothes/and come dancing" ("Para Olga"), and with him as guru-dancing master, the uplifted, rhythmed, ecstatic dance of hippy idealism—even in the midst of the prevailing view of America as a sad, grey, police-state—seems not only feasible but imperative. Laffing Water's strength is not merely his own internal conviction, but the force he manifests on the world around him with his work—and life.

Conclusion

Gary Snyder in an article, "Why Tribe," written for the first issue of *Buzoku* in 1967, talks about the evolution of a "tribe" in the U.S. and Europe since the end of World War I, a tribe that evolved as a reaction against the insanity of the contemporary psychotic tech-world. The "outsiders"—to use Colin Wilson's term—banded together and became an international "supra-nation" united by a common vision and need to dip into the East to find what the West didn't and couldn't give—a structural world-view with its base-points not in external-to-man-production-consumption schedules (the machine given priority over man) but in a world-view made for the purpose of man-exploration, experimentation, amplification.

Snyder, one of the original Beat Generation, is more relevant today than he was fifteen years ago. He is a genuine *guru*. . . . a seeker-after-light who has found it. I remember one time last year when he left a volume of manuscript poems he had been reading at my place and I went over to bring the volume back to him. I found him with a green silk cloth wrapped around his head, in the middle of meditation. Meditation—the ways of Zen, Vajrayana, Yoga, Shamanism, Psychedelics—is a part of Snyder's personal fiber. He radiates the calm and gentleness, the freshness and ease of manner that he speaks of as the mark of a modern "outsider" tribesman. Snyder has gotten where Levy, Simon, Cauble and the other undergrounders have been trying to go.

Miguel Grinberg, Argentinian editor of *Eco Contemporaneo*, one of the leaders in the New Solidarity movement, feels that the older Beats have been much more successful, more sincere in their "quests" and "conversions." When he visited another one of the original Beats, Alan Ginsberg, he told me, "When I got there for dinner, there were two other 'guests.' Whatever they had to eat—eggs, cheese, bread—they automatically divided so that I'd have my equal share. It was an automatic, unconscious act of 'sharing.'"

Of course the Beats were the sons of the Depression, and the Hippies the sons of the Post World War II Boom. The Beats were still "linear," the Hippies are "curvilinear," the Beats were "sequential," the Hippies are "instantaneous," the Beats were "natural," the Hippies are "electronic." Somehow the Beats, emerging from the West when the West was in a moment of bankruptcy (1929–39), did not have "Occidentalism" (the need for regimented, externalized, ego-fattening "control") that deeply imprinted on their psyches. The occidental force-field had broken down momentarily, and they were able to break through into a soft, internal revolution. Then too, the Megamachine had not been as thoroughly developed in the 1950's as it has been in the 1960's. The U.S. is still *in the process* of total "cybernetization."

Levy implies something of this change in his "Rectal Eye Vision Number 7—for Allen Ginsberg"—the poem where in he calls Ginsberg "among the most holy & sacred men in this desert." Levy aspires to Ginsberg's sanctity, but the nature of the desert has changed, the pressure "out there" has grown. The poet-*guru* born into the increasingly pressurized world of mind-control has increasing trouble detaching himself and floating in the void of unselfed selfness:

> how many survived   waiting   hiding
> centuries piled upon centuries waiting
>   for the Day of Love to arrive & instead

they are greeted by the facist princes &
          the war lords
Ulysees, hitler, mussolini, franco, stalin, johnson
eisenhower, trujillo, batista etc etc etc the
names always spell/IMPOTENT BRAIN WAVES &
          UNCONTROLLED DEATH

The underground poets are, really, the most sensitive, vocal, clairvoyant *witnesses* of the fact of the increased impermeability and automation of U.S. culture. They haven't stopped crying in the wilderness, but the wilderness—programmed, automatic, in a process of continuous acceleration of its own mechanization-qualities—is slowly closing in on them and silencing them not only by repression and supression but, even more fatally, by indifference.

At the same time another factor, totally apart from the increased political "control mechanisms" of U.S. society, is responsible for the isolation and alienation of these poets: the fact that they are being caught in the time-gap between print and media cultures. There is a great deal of similarity between a Levy or a Krech or Simon and a Leonard Cohen, Buffy St. Marie or Pete Seeger. . . . but if you move out of print into records-TV-films, although all that essentially has changed is the "how" of presentation, still the "how" changes the whole dimension of communication.

It might be, however, that Kryss, RJS and Levy are right, that there is some inherent conflict between the raw primitive search for tribalism, selfness, cosmic unity, and processed media reality, that the underground represents one last "open-air" impulse in the "developed countries," to escape from mediafication which in itself is merely one more aspect of a more comprehensive, more all-inclusive environment control. The "developed countries" are on the brink of a kind of "artificialization" which threatens to separate them from elemental reality and consequently alienate them further from the reality of the rest of the world "out there," the third world. . . . a world barely beginning to be *able* to process reality at all.

The underground in the U.S. has been the U.S.'s contribution to the New Solidarity, and the undergrounders have been able to share in the mystique of Latin America, Asia, Africa. . . . not viewing these realities processed, but in the raw, still finding human elements in themselves that correspond to the realities of the humanity "out there." The rest of the U.S., covered by the multiple domes of media processing, becomes increasingly cut off from "out there" *and* from the elements of reality not included inside the media domes themselves— for example, the Negro or Mexican reality.

Since the Renaissance the dominant characteristic of intellectual history has been increased technification. In a way science and technology have been "deified," and the future of mankind has been put under the magic protection of these new gods. Of course this technification has been worldwide to a great extent, but has reached its apogee in the occident. The "realities" of rural India, say, or Siam or much of Africa are something else again.

The changes in psychic reality accompanying the changes in technological reality have separated the U.S. and the rest of the developed world from much of contemporary mankind and much of what might be termed mankind's "non-technological past." The application of technology to the human "condition" has forced much of the "non-technological" store of human characteristics into the background. Man has been sanitized, deodorized, fixed into schedules and unit-time-production plans, and the rich store of the primitive (or even primate) past has been ignored, paralyzed by the "media," separated from the dollar-trapped necessities of the "pure consumer." We are only fourteen years away from the subconscious-controlling world of *1984*.

The Hippy impulse has been one last-ditch attempt on the part of the young permeable to shaggy, uncomfortable, primitive, unprocessed, unscheduled, dream-nightmare, skin-hair reality. And it seems to have failed.

Perhaps the whole dream of an instantaneous drug-based Utopia was too "American" to begin with. The "content," perhaps, came from "outside" (the East, Africa, the American Indian), but the whole methodology had too much to do with Henry Ford and TV dinners. Instant pudding, instant rice, instant oats. . . . and instant mysticism, perhaps they're all too much a part of the same non-human machine-culture.

What Krech or Simon or Levy all wanted was "enlightenment." Only unlike a Snyder or a Ginsberg, "asceticism" as such has played a small part in their lives. They have been on the borders, the fringe of affluent society, but have never dropped out. . . . over the edge.

Jainism, Buddhism, even primitive Christianity all stress the necessity of a long process of austerity before "enlightenment" can be attained. The senses are all tamed, subdued, the "self" dies and is reborn on the other side of "self-interest." Only the process is never easy or fast—certainly never instantaneous, never "Add drugs, stir and wait for five minutes before experiencing."

Perhaps this is the real weak point of the whole instant mysticism of contemporary U.S. poetry. We are all mystics who want our three squares a day, our record players, our mimeos, our "pot." Only affluent-mysticism. . . .? Is it any more, really than a surface imitation (or even parody) of the Hindu fakir or the Burmese bonze?

At the same time the new political activism, the conversion from mystical to armed quest may be nothing more than another surface imitation of a new, growing current in the Third World—that of armed revolution. The young American, of course, even though he is more at home with a gun than a vision (the gun a much more intimate and familiar part of his whole pragmatic world-view), still is so far "contained" inside the structures of 1984-ism that he is unaware of the insincerity of his own pose, stance, gestures. And then too "Che" might be not merely a forced symbol of self-deceptive romanticism, but more important a lesson in the fact that even the Third World is fast falling under the spell of occidental control-mechanisms.

The fight of contemporary U.S. underground mystics against "the system" is substantially different from previous "outsider" (primitive) fights against other "systems." The present day undergrounders are *not* primitive Christians fighting against imperial Rome. Imperial North America is a very different kind of imperialism based on very different control approaches.

"The system" does not stop at physical control, but extends throughout the whole gamut of human emotions, goals, fears. The Hippies have been trained from birth to be part of not only the producer-consumer cycle, but also part of the "image-making" process, the star is born, gotta-make-it need to "succeed" in something, somehow. The media has turned the whole population into aspiring "stars" who are more concerned about "image" than "inner reality." Not only does this psychically tie an individual to "consumption," it also prevents any real break with "things" and keeps him forever on stage worrying about the "reviews."

The whole Hippie movement has been a kind of masquerade. The land of Coca Cola, Ford, GM, U.S. Steel and IBM suddenly went gypsy, Hindu, Buddhist, Indian. . . . wild. Everyone's best friend was a *guru,* logic was discarded and the whole youth population turned on looking at light shows projected on coffee house walls—while under "the influence." The easily identifiable enemies, of course, were THE MASTERS OF WAR and then—more diffusely—the "Establishment." And the New Saints. . . . .? Us, the bearded, long-haired, earringed, booted nomadic dropouts.

Only these same dropouts had already been programmed by the Megamachine. They'd been programmed in their cribs, during their childhood, during all their early teens. . . . not merely with "but" and "conform," but—more important—"be beautiful." Luxury consumption had turned everyone into a Marlboro Ad or the "Last of the Big Spenders," or Billy the Kid, or the Aga Kahn. The reaction to the time-clocked, steel-edged manufacturing system did not really come from the *I Ching* or the *Vedas,* but from the Pepsi-Generation mentality that had pushed a whole segment of the U.S. population away from Puritan work-mystique austerity to opulent orientalism, where you could buy Frankincense and Myrrh at your corner Psychedelic Shoppe. Instead of being anti-materialistic—which did produce results in the Beats— the Hippie movement was basically an *extension* and *glorification* of materialism—facile, instantaneous, and ecstatic.

The underground poets are ideal witnesses to the results—so far. The older poets like Higgins or Morris played it safe, the younger ones like Krech, Simon, Laffing Water, Sharon Asselin, RJS, D. A. Levy, whenever they did break out of the "control world" found that they couldn't really handle the "out there."

One suspects that the 1970's will be the decade of Counter-Hippyism, that the pot bonfires will get bigger, the militia and national guard and the local police get tougher (and more numerous), the crackdowns and trials get more frequent, faster and less concerned with the "due process of law."

But then no "movement" ever settles anything anyhow. The Christians triumphed, Rome fell, and then came Renaissance Christianity. Reform and revolt must remain an inherent evolutionary process, and the dialectic of action and counteraction must continue to prevent any definitive stabilization of "man" into one solid state. Flux, after all, is the necessary ambience of any movement toward betterment.

The Underground remains as witnesses to change. Even if they themselves do not initiate or continue change, they remain the last "sensors" on the fringe of the controlled world who can still report the progress (or decline) of the changes inside this world.